Practical
Exercises
for ECDL

Syllabus 4.0

Jackie Sherman

Practical Exercises for ECDL

Syllabus 4.0

IMPORTANT NOTICE

This book, which has been approved by the ECDL Foundation, includes exercise items intended to help ECDL candidates in their training for ECDL. These exercises are not ECDL certification tests and are not guarantees of passing the official ECDL test. For information about authorised ECDL Test Centres in different national territories, please refer to the ECDL Foundation website at www.ecdl.com

---

An imprint of **Pearson Education**

London · Boston · Indianapolis · New York · Mexico City · Toronto · Sydney · Tokyo
Singapore · Hong Kong · Cape Town · Madrid · Paris · Amsterdam · Munich · Milan

Pearson Education Limited
Edinburgh Gate
Harlow
Essex CM20 2JE
England

and Associated Companies throughout the world

Visit us on the World Wide Web at:
www.pearsoned.co.uk

First published 2006

© Jackie Sherman 2006

The questions and exercises found in this book have been written especially for it. You can find official sample questions on the EDCL website: www.ecdl.com

European Computer Driving Licence, ECDL and Stars Device, ECDL, International Computer Driving Licence, ICDL International Computer Driving Licence and logo, ICDL, and e-Citizen are trade marks of The European Computer Driving Licence Foundation Limited ("ECDL-F") in Ireland and other countries.

Pearson Education Ltd is an entity independent of ECDL-F and is not associated with ECDL-F in any manner. This courseware publication may be used to assist candidates to prepare for the ECDL examination. Neither ECDL-F nor Pearson Education Ltd warrants that the use of this courseware publication will ensure passing of the ECDL. Use of the ECDL-F Approved Courseware logo on this courseware publication signifies that it has been independently reviewed and approved by ECDL-F as complying with the following standard:

> *Technical compliance with the learning objectives of ECDL syllabus 4.0.*

The material contained in this courseware publication has not been reviewed for technical accuracy and does not guarantee that candidates will pass the ECDL examination. Any and all assessment items and/or performance-based exercises contained in this courseware publication relate solely to this publication and do not constitute or imply certification by ECDL-F in respect of the ECDL examination or any other ECDL-F test.

For details on sitting the ECDL examination and other ECDL-F tests in your country, please contact your country's National ECDL/ICDL designated Licensee or visit ECDL-F's web site at www.ecdl.com.

Candidates using this courseware publication must be registered with the National Licensee, before undertaking the ECDL examination. Without a valid registration, the ECDL examination cannot be undertaken and no ECDL certificate, nor any other form of recognition, can be given to a candidate. Registration should be undertaken with your country's National ECDL/ICDL designated Licensee at any Approved ECDL Test Centre.

ECDL Syllabus 4.0 is the official syllabus of the ECDL certification programme at the data of approval of this courseware publication.

ISBN 10: 0-13-147958-X
ISBN 13: 978-0-13-147958-6

British Library Cataloguing-in-Publication Data
A catalogue record for this book is available from the British Library

Library of Congress Cataloging-in-Publication Data
A catalog record for this book is available from the Library of Congress

10 9 8 7 6 5 4 3
10 09 08 07 06

Typeset in 10/13 pt Stone Serif by 30
Printed by Bell & Bain Ltd., Glasgow

The publisher's policy is to use paper manufactured from sustainable forests.

Contents

PART 1   QUESTIONS AND EXERCISES   1

PART 2 MODEL ANSWERS 157

Introduction

Learning to use a computer, as with any new skill, requires two things: finding out what is involved and then practising until you are confident you can perform the tasks successfully. Passing the ECDL demands even more practice, as most Test Centres now offer online tests where you have to demonstrate in a limited time that you can carry out all the basic tasks expected of competent computer users.

Although there are many books on the market that teach you how to use a computer, very few contain exercises that encourage you to practise what you have learned. However, to pass the ECDL you need to be sure you can use the various applications fully. That is why this book has been written. When read in conjunction with the ECDL Complete Coursebooks and 'How to Pass' Workbooks by Brendan Munnelly and Paul Holden, you can now learn how to create documents, spreadsheets, charts, presentations and databases, use browsers and e-mail systems, and then check that you have understood and gained the necessary skills by working through the relevant exercises at your own pace.

About the author

Jackie Sherman has been involved in teaching and assessing IT courses at further education colleges since 1996. She also trains staff in an education department and writes courses for distance learning colleges. Her online activities include being on the National Tutor Database for LearnDirect and answering IT questions for the YouCanDoIT column for www.laterlife.com. Jackie is ECDL-qualified and is the author of two successful IT books.

Acknowledgements

We are grateful to the following for permission to reproduce copyright material:

Microsoft® Office screenshots reprinted by permission from Microsoft Corporation; Model answers in Chapter 7: Exercise 1 from www.bbc.co.uk/weather/5day.shtml?id= 3263, British Broadcasting Corporation; Exercise 2 from www.laterlife. com/, Laterlife.Com Limited; Exercise 3 from www.waitrose.com/ online_shopping/ index.asp, Waitrose; Exercise 3 from www.Iceland.co. uk/, Iceland; Exercise 4 from www. mkisc.org.uk/, Rob Stubbs and the Milton Keynes Ice Skating Club; Exercise 5 from www.google.com/ search?hl=en&ie=UTF-8&q=skating+rinks&btnG= Google+Search, Google Inc.; Exercise 6 from www.drumaneeaquatics.co.uk, Drumanee Aquatics; Exercise 7 from www.nrm.org.uk/html/home_pb/menu.asp, reproduced courtesy of the National Railway Museum, © Trustees of the Science Museum, 2004; Exercise 10 from www.toysrus.co.uk, Toys R Us Ltd.; Exercise 13 from www.guardian.co.uk/, © The Guardian; Exercise 14 from www.firstchoice.co.uk/holidaydeals/index.cfm?step=holiday_ search_ results&page=3, First Choice Holidays plc.

In some instances we have been unable to trace the owners of copyright material, and we would appreciate any information that would enable us to do so.

1

Questions and exercises

Each section in Part 1 contains between 20 and 30 questions or exercises designed to test your knowledge of the ECDL syllabus. These increase in complexity as you work through the section. At the beginning of each exercise, the main skills required to complete it are listed and the following symbol ⟨ECDL⟩ refers you to the relevant section of the ECDL syllabus in case you need further guidance.

Model answers to most of the questions and exercises can be found in Part 2.

Good luck!

The seven sections within this first part of the book relate to the following ECDL modules:

Module number

1. Concepts of information technology
2. Using the computer and managing files
3. Word processing
4. Spreadsheets
5. Databases
6. Presentation
7. Information and communication

Concepts of information technology

This module tests your knowledge of the basic facts about computers, whether you know your rights and responsibilities as a computer user and how computers are used in everyday life. You will also be asked some general questions about the Internet and e-mail.

Subjects covered in this section:

Advanced questions   **ECDL module**

5.	E-mail	**1.5.2**
6.	Copyright	**1.8.1**
7.	Portable computers	**1.1.2**
8.	Hardware	**1.2.4**
9.	RAM	**1.2.2**
10.	Formatting disks	**1.2.6**
11.	Shareware	**1.8.1**
12.	Pointing devices	**1.2.3**
13.	Modems	**1.4.4**
14.	'Zipping'	**1.2.6**
15.	Storing information	**1.2.2**

1. Name a common desktop publishing application and explain its purpose.

2. In businesses, computers are often networked. Give three reasons why this has advantages for the organization.

3. What is the reason for using passwords on computers? Why do you see ***** when you type your password?

4. List three ways in which a hospital might use a computer to improve the delivery of health care.

5. Explain the purpose of keeping backup copies of files.

6. Name two sources of computer viruses. What steps can you take to reduce the risk of catching viruses?

7. What is the main purpose of the Data Protection Act? Give one reason why each of the following organizations might keep personal data on computer:

    a) bank
    b) school or college
    c) doctor's surgery.

8. How does system software differ from application software? Give one example of each.

9. What is the difference between the Internet and the World Wide Web?

10. Explain the term GUI. Give two advantages of GUI compared with earlier methods of working with computers.

11. Name three different means of communicating using the telephone network. Which method(s) require the use of a computer?

12. What might you find in the i) A: drive, ii) C: drive and iii) D: drive of a computer?

13. Name the four main stages in the development of software systems. What is the role of a programmer?

14. What term is used to describe the setting up of a business on the Internet? List three advantages and three disadvantages of shopping online.

15. Give two reasons for using floppy diskettes for storing files.

ADVANCED QUESTIONS

1. Which five steps can you take to ensure that you work safely with your computer?

2. What is a CPU? How is its speed measured?

3. Name three activities that can be carried out when using online banking facilities.

4. Describe the difference between laser and inkjet printers.

5. Give three reasons for using e-mail rather than the post when sending messages.

6. Why does copyright matter when searching for pictures on the Internet?

7. What is a common name for a portable computer? Describe three ways in which it differs from a desktop computer.

8. List two input and two output hardware devices in a computer system. Select one output device and describe briefly how it works.

9. What does RAM stand for? In which two ways does it differ from ROM?

10. Explain how to format a floppy diskette. How often should you format the hard disk? Select one option:
    a) once a week
    b) once a year
    c) only on special occasions
    d) you cannot do this – you must return the computer to your supplier.

11. What is shareware? What is the difference between shareware and freeware?

12. Why are pointing devices used with a computer? List four different types of pointing device and describe briefly how one of these works.

13. Why would you use a modem? How do modems work, and what is their current top speed?

14. Explain the term 'zipping'.

15. What measurement units are appropriate for the following (select from gigabytes (GB), megabytes (MB) and bytes):
    a) hard disk
    b) RAM
    c) CD-ROM
    d) floppy diskette.

MODULE 2

Using the computer and managing files

This module will help you to check that you can give your machine instructions, that you understand the desktop and that you can work with Microsoft Windows. You will also be tested on your knowledge of how to work safely with a computer and how to organize your work into folders.

Subjects covered in this section:

Introductory questions		ECDL module
1.	Shutting down your computer	2.1.1
2.	File types	2.3.3
3.	Using the **Help** menu	2.1.2
4.	Changing the size of a window	2.2.2
5.	Working with printers	2.5.1
6.	Restarting your machine	2.1.1
7.	Exploring your computer	2.1.2
8.	Exploring folders	2.3.2
9.	Using Find	2.3.6
10.	Zipping	2.3.7

Exercises		ECDL module
1–2	Creating files and folders, renaming and deleting folders	2.1.3, 2.3.2, 2.3.3 and 2.3.5
3–4	Copying, moving, renaming and deleting files	2.3.3, 2.3.4 and 2.3.5
5–6	Working with multiple files, using Find	2.3.4 and 2.3.6
7–8	Saving a file into a folder	2.1.3
9–10	Using Print Screen and printing a file	2.1.2 and 2.5.2

1. Describe the process for shutting down your computer. Why is it wrong to simply turn off the power?

2. **a)** Name two common image file types.
   b) Identify which types of files have the following extensions:
   .txt   .htm   .xls   .doc

3. Use the Help menu to provide details of where the calculator is located on your computer.

4. Explain how to change the size of a window on the desktop.

5. What is the name of your default printer? If you were also linked to a different printer, how would you change the default?

6. Describe three different methods for restarting your machine if it freezes.

7. From the desktop, find out and note down your computer's operating system, RAM and processor.

8. Open the Recycle Bin or My Documents folder, reorganize the contents to display full details, and note down three different types of file that it contains and the dates the files were deleted or modified.

9. Use the Find facility to locate any file or folder named Notepad. Note down the number of items listed and the main folder location.

10. Describe the steps to take in order to compress or zip several large files.

You need to know how to:

▶ Create a folder

▶ Open a word processing application and start, name and save a new document.

▶ Create subfolders inside a folder

▶ Rename or delete folders

2

Exercise 1

1. Open My Documents (or a floppy disk if preferred) either on the desktop or within Windows Explorer.

2. Create a folder and name it **Numbers**.

3. Inside the **Numbers** folder, create two subfolders and name them **Large** and **Medium**.

4. In Word, start a new document. Type the word **Eleven** and then save the file with the same name. Note the default location where you are saving the file. Close the file.

5. Create and save five more files named **Three**, **Seven**, **Two**, **Four** and **Six**. Make sure all files are closed and then either close or minimize Word.

6. Re-open the **Numbers** folder and rename the two sub-folders. They should now be named **Even** and **Odd**.

 Module 2, sections 1.3, 3.2 and 3.3

Exercise 2

1. Within My Documents or on a floppy disk, create a folder named **Food**.

2. Inside the folder, create three sub-folders and name these **Fruit**, **Veg** and **Salad**.

3. Open Word, create five files and save them with the following names: **Lemon**, **Carrot**, **Potato**, **Apple** and **Blackcurrant**. Either type the file name in the document before saving or save blank files. Close all the files and either close or minimize Word.

4. Return to your folders and rename **Veg** so that it becomes **Vegetables**.

5. Delete the **Salad** sub-folder.

 Module 2, sections 1.3, 3.2 and 3.3

You will need to know how to:

‣ Move files into folders

‣ Copy files into folders

‣ Rename or delete files

Exercise 3 1. Locate the file named **Three** and move it into the **Odd** sub-folder.

2. Locate files named **Seven** and **Eleven** and move them into the same sub-folder.

3. Locate the files named **Two, Four** and **Six** and move them into the **Even** sub-folder.

4. Copy the file named **Seven** into the **Numbers** folder.

5. Re-name this file **Number 7**.

6. Re-open the **Odd** folder and delete the original file named **Seven**.

 Module 2, sections 3.3, 3.4 and 3.5

Exercise 4 1. Locate the **Lemon** file and move it into the **Fruit** folder.

2. Locate **Apple** and **Blackcurrant** and add these to the **Fruit** folder.

3. Rename **Blackcurrant** so that it is named **Blackberry**.

4. Now locate the **Carrot** and **Potato** files and move them into the **Vegetables** folder.

5. Place a copy of **Apple** in the **Vegetables** folder and rename the file **Leek**.

 Module 2, sections 3.3, 3.4 and 3.5

You will need to know how to:

▶ Move or copy more than one file at the same time

▶ Find files or folders

Exercise 5 1. Use the Find facility to locate the **Number 7** file created earlier.

2. Note down the full details of file type, size and date it was last modified.

3. Now open the **Even** sub-folder.

4. Select all the files and move them together into the **Numbers** folder.

5. Delete the **Even** sub-folder.

6. Finally, open the **Odd** sub-folder and copy all its contents into the **Numbers** folder.

 Module 2, sections 3.4 and 3.6

Exercise 6 1. Use the Find facility to locate the **Potato** file. Note down its size, file type and the date it was last modified.

2. Open the **Vegetables** sub-folder and move **Leek** and **Potato** together into the **Food** folder.

3. Copy **Carrot** into the **Food** folder and rename this file **Carrot tops**.

4. Delete the **Vegetables** sub-folder together with any files it still contains.

 Module 2, sections 3.4 and 3.6

You will need to know how to:

▶ Save a file into a folder

Exercise 7 1. Open Word and start a new, blank document.

2. Save the file with the name Ten into the Numbers folder.

3. Now create a new file named Orange and save it into the Fruit subfolder.

4. On the desktop or within your file management program, check that the file Ten is listed inside the Numbers folder. Re-name the file Ten times table.

5. Now check that Orange is inside the Fruit subfolder. Copy it into the Food folder and re-name the copy Orange blossom.

6. Locate the file Carrot tops and delete it completely.

7. Finally, create a new folder named Managing My Files and move the following four files into it at the same time: Lemon, Apple, Orange and Blackberry.

 Module 2, section 1.3

Exercise 8 1. In My Documents or on a floppy disk, create the following three folders: German, Italian and French.

2. Inside the Italian folder, create two subfolders named Male and Female.

3. In Word, create a file named Gatto. Save it into the Male subfolder.

4. Now create the following five files and save them into the folders shown in brackets: Casa (Female), Libro (Male), Regazzo (Female), Haus (French) and Tavola (Female).

5. On the desktop or within your file management program, open the Female subfolder. Locate the file Regazzo and move it into the Male subfolder.

6. Copy Gatto into the French folder and rename the file Chat.

7. Copy the file Tavola into the German folder and rename the file Tafel.

8. Finally, move the file named Haus into the German folder.

 Module 2, section 1.3

You will need to know how to:

◗ Use the Print Screen facility

◗ Print a file

2

Exercise 9 1. Open the file named Gatto.

2. Type the following words: The Italian word for cat is gatto.

3. Update your file to save the changes and then close the file.

4. Now open the file named Haus and type the following text: The German word for house is Haus.

5. Save these words and then close the file.

6. On the desktop or within Windows Explorer, open the Male subfolder, and then open the file named Gatto.

7. Print one copy and then close the file.

8. Locate and open the file named Haus and print two copies.

9. Close the file and Word.

10. Open the Male folder and use Print Screen to take and print a picture of the contents.

 Module 2, sections 1.2 and 5.2

Exercise 10 1. Locate and open the file named Orange.

2. Type the following words: The word orange means the same in English and French.

3. Save these changes and close the file.

4. Open the Managing My Files folder and move Orange into the folder named French.

5. Now open Orange and print one copy.

6. Close the file and Word.

7. Open the French folder and use Print Screen to take and print a picture of its contents

 Module 2, sections 1.2 and 5.2

MODULE

Word processing

In this module you will test your word processing skills. In the ECDL exam you will need to show that you can create, save and print documents that are formatted attractively, and that you are able to incorporate images or items brought in from elsewhere and can move or edit these as appropriate. You will also be tested on the various features that are available to help you work efficiently with long documents.

Subjects covered in this section:

Advanced exercises		**ECDL module**
1–2	Headers and footers; inserting a page break; printing selected pages	**3.3.3 and 3.6.2**
3	Inserting symbols	**3.2.1**
4	Using the **Insert** menu; saving files into a new folder	**3.3.3**
5–6	Working with Clip Art	**3.4.2**
7	Change case; hanging indents	**3.3.1 and 3.3.2**
8	Adding borders and shading	**3.3.2**
9	Creating and editing tables	**3.4.1**
10	Applying an AutoFormat to a table	**3.4.1**
11–12	Working with tabs; applying a font colour	**3.3.1 and 3.3.2**
13	Working with styles and templates	**3.3.1 and 3.3.3**
14–15	Setting up a Mail Merge	**3.5.1**

EXERCISES 1 AND 2

You will need to know how to:

▶ Create a simple document

▶ Make amendments

▶ Save a file

▶ Print a copy

Exercise 1 1. Open your word processing application and, on a blank page, enter the following text in capitals:

SURFACE FEEDERS

2. Press **Enter** twice and type the following text, only pressing **Enter** when you are ready to start the second paragraph:

All the fish found 'just under the surface' have a perfectly straight back, which allows their upturned mouths to get right up to the surface. Foods which float for some time are ideal for these fish.

A common surface feeder is the Glass Catfish. This fish is a native of India and is very active and lively. It can reach a size of about 5 cm and is best kept in shoals.

3. Check the text for errors (i.e. proof-read). To correct mistakes, click on the error with the mouse or use your arrow keys to move the cursor and delete or insert letters or spaces as necessary.

4. Save the file as **Surface Feeders** onto a floppy disk, or into the My Documents folder on the hard disk or, if working on networked computers, into a designated area.

5. Print one copy.

6. Now make the following changes:
   ● After upturned mouths insert the following text:
     (ideal for scooping up floating foods, usually insects)
   ● Replace the name **Glass Catfish** with **Zebra Danio**.

7. Add your own name on a new line at the end of the text and print a copy of the amended document.

8. Update the file to save the changes.

9. Close the document.

 Module 3, sections 1.1 and 6.2

Exercise 2 1. Start a new document and enter the following text:

THE POTENTIAL OF MUSIC

Teachers generally provide a stimulating environment for children in their classes, with respect to sight and touch, but more can be done. Other experiences may be overlooked. One of the senses which can be educated quite easily is hearing. Sounds are all around us in the secondary school and with careful structuring they can even become organized sounds – music.

Children make sounds all the time – they talk, shout, cry, scream or sing. A good way to focus on sounds is to tell stories needing 'sound effects', such as those of police cars, ambulances, trains or ghosts.

2. Proof-read and correct any errors.

3. Save as The Potential of Music.

4. Print one copy.

5. Now make the following amendments:
   - Change secondary school to infants.
   - Delete the phrase: but more can be done.
   - Insert the following text after … focus on sounds is:
     to use rhymes and poems and

6. Add your name at the end of the document and print one copy.

7. Save the changes you have made to update the file.

8. Close the document.

 Module 3, sections 1.1 and 6.2

EXERCISE 3

You will need to know how to:

▸ Open a file saved previously

▸ Save a file as a different version of the original

1. Open the file Surface Feeders.

2. Insert a third paragraph:

The Siamese Fighting Fish is hardy, but you can only have one male in a tank otherwise fighting will break out. If you want to see it display, put a mirror at the side of the tank. Aquarium-cultivated strains usually have bodies and fins of one colour, apart from the Cambodia Fighter that has a cream body and coloured fins.

3. Change the heading to: FIGHTING FISH

4. Proof-read and correct any mistakes.

5. Save this as a new file with the filename Siamese Fighter.

6. Print one copy.

7. Close the document.

8. Open the file The Potential of Music.

9. Add the following paragraph:

   One activity teachers can try is to sit the group in a circle. Everyone claps three times, then leaves a space equivalent to three more claps, and then everyone claps three times again. How the gap is filled is up to the teacher, but you could alternate between 'oohs' and 'aahs'.

10. Change the heading to: MUSIC GAMES.

11. Proof-read and correct any mistakes.

12. Save this as a new file with the file name Clapping.

13. Print one copy.

14. Close the document.

 Module 3, section 1.1

EXERCISES 4 AND 5

You will need to know how to:

▶ Use the automatic spelling and grammar checker

Exercise 4 1. Start a new document and type the following text as shown, retaining spelling mistakes to the words quarter, blood, arteries and oxygen:

Heart Disease

Heart disease causes a quarrter of all deaths in Britain. It is the biggest killer of middle-aged men in the developed world.

You need a healthy heart to pump bloood around your body, and heart muscle needs food and oxygen for it to keep contracting. These are carried in the coronary arteries. If the arnteries get blocked, then it can cause heart disease. The risk increases if you smoke, become overweight or take no exercise.

A total blockage or thrombosis can cause a heart attack. Here the supply of oxygeen is cut off, there are severe pains in the chest and the affected part of the heart is damaged.

2. Proof-read and use the automatic spelling and grammar checker to correct any mistakes.

3. Save the file with the file name Heart Disease.

4. Print one copy.

5. Now make the following amendments:

   - Change the title to read: The Problems of Heart Disease
   - Delete the final sentence in paragraph two beginning The risk ... .
   - Add the following sentence to the start of paragraph three:
     The artery wall can become rough and this can cause the blood to clot and block the vessel.

6. Update the file to save the changes.

7. Print one copy.

8. Close the document.

 Module 3, section 6.1

Exercise 5 1. Start a new document and enter the title of a favourite book or film followed by the word Uncorrected.

2. Type out two paragraphs outlining the main story.

3. Leave any spelling or grammar mistakes uncorrected – if necessary, add a few extra letters to some words to create mistakes – and save the document with the book or film title as the file name.

4. Print a copy of the uncorrected document.

5. Now correct all the mistakes, using the spelling or grammar checker where possible.

6. Change the word Uncorrected to Corrected in the main title.

7. Save the file as a new version with the file name Book/Film Title 2.

8. Print a copy of the corrected document.

9. Close the document.

 Module 3, section 6.1

You will need to know how to:

▸ Select text

▸ Format text

▸ Save files as different file types

Exercise 6 1. Open the file Heart Disease.

2. Make the title bold and underlined.

3. Select the complete text and increase the font size.

4. Select the final paragraph and format it to italic.

5. Save the changes.

6. Add a new paragraph, formatted to Arial, 14 point, underlined:

     You can take care of your heart by eating more poultry and fish. Cut down on fried foods and red meat and always eat plenty of fruit and vegetables.

7. Save and print a copy of the document.

8. Close the document.

9. Reopen and save as plain text, changing the name to Heart Disease – New type.

10. Close and then reopen the file, making sure you search for plain text files. Print a copy and compare it to the document you printed earlier.

 Module 3, sections 1.1, 2.2 and 3.1

Exercise 7 1. Start a new document and enter the following text:

     ONE POT WONDER
     (Serves 2 – 3)

     4 lamb chops
     700g peeled and diced carrots, potatoes and swedes
     pinch of dried oregano
     15ml tomato puree

     Preheat the oven to gas mark 7. Tip vegetables into a shallow ovenproof dish and arrange the lamb chops over the top. Sprinkle over the herbs, season then roast in the oven for 15 minutes.

Mix the tomato puree with a cupful of hot water and pour over the chops and vegetables. Continue cooking for another 20 minutes.

2. Proof-read and save as One Pot Wonder.

3. Print a copy of the recipe.

4. Select the title and format to bold.

5. Select the list of ingredients and format to italic.

6. Select the instructions, increase the font size and apply a different font, e.g. Times New Roman or Courier.

7. Select the title and add a double underline via the **Format | Font** menu.

8. Save these changes and print a copy of the amended recipe.

9. Save a second version of the file as a plain text file with the name OPWplain.

10. Close the document.

 Module 3, sections 1.1, 2.2 and 3.1

EXERCISES 8 AND 9

You will need to know how to:

▶ Align text

▶ Amend line spacing

Exercise 8 1. The following items are available on a hotel breakfast menu:

fruit juice or cereal
fried egg, sausage, bacon, fried tomatoes, fried bread
grilled kippers
toast and marmalade
tea, hot chocolate or coffee

2. Type out a menu with the title Breakfast at Hotel Belle Vue. The food items should be arranged as five separate courses with at least one line in-between each item, and all text should be centred on the page.

3. Format the title so that it stands out, e.g. increase the font size, make it bold or underlined, etc.

4. Separate the courses with symbols, e.g. """"" or +++++.

5. At the bottom of the menu, enter the following text, left aligned:

   Breakfast will be served from 7.30 – 9.00 a.m. Please note that some items on the menu may change according to availability as we like to offer the freshest ingredients in our meals.

6. Add today's date at the top of the menu, right-aligned.

7. Save as Breakfast and print a copy.

8. Double space the final paragraph, left align the date and then print a copy of the amended document.

9. Update the file to save these changes, and then close.

 Module 3, section 3.2

Exercise 9 1. Create the following document, proof-read it, and save as Viruses:

   Catching the Fever

   Viruses are an unpleasant fact of computing life we could all do without. However, by being aware of the nature of the problem you can guard against the risk of PC infections.

   If you've yet to be infected by a computer virus, you're in a dwindling minority. There are now so many viruses in circulation that it's almost impossible to use a PC for any length of time and not encounter one. Cutting through the hype about viruses isn't easy though, particularly when some computer users add to it by forwarding bogus virus alerts to all and sundry.

2. Centre the title and format it as bold.

3. Fully justify the main text.

4. Change the line spacing of the first paragraph to 1.5, and double space the second.

5. Add the date at the bottom of the document, right-aligned.

6. Apply an alternative font to the whole document.

7. Increase the font size of the title text to 14.

8. Save these changes and print a copy. Then close the file.

 Module 3, section 3.2

You will need to know how to:

▶ Indent paragraphs

▶ Use the **Edit | Replace** menu

1. Create the following document, proof-read and correct any errors.

   IT'S OK TO GIVE ORDERS

   Good behaviour in kids is required not as a whim of parents but to make practical living easier. Unlike parents of the Victorian era, we do not need pointless obedience, such as brushing one's hair before tea, but we do ask kids to co-operate to make life easier.

   When kids don't co-operate, the parents find their life inconvenienced. Soft parents will soon find they are being given the run-around. However much they want to give in and not inhibit their children's creativity, these parents find they are very angry and tired of the troubles this causes, and attempt to restore order. Feeling steamed up, they may lash out and discipline their kids in a way that they and the child know is somewhat out of control. This is bad for everyone concerned and there are more successful ways to give orders.

2. Save as Orders and print a copy.

3. Indent the first paragraph by 1 cm from the left margin.

4. Using the **Edit | Replace** menu, replace the word kids with the word children wherever it occurs (four times).

5. Left-align the title and underline the word OK.

6. Add the following text as a new paragraph, indented by 1.5 cm from both the left and right margins:

   Be clear in your own mind: It's not a request or open to debate, it's a demand which you have a right to make.

   Make good contact: Stop what you are doing, go up close to the child and get her to look at you.

   Be direct: Say, "I want you to .... now. Do you understand?" Make sure you get a "yes" or "no" answer.

7. Save these changes and print a final copy.

 Module 3, sections 2.5 and 3.2

You will need to know how to:

◗ Check a document in Print Preview

◗ Change margins

1. Create the following document, proof-read it and save as Gardening:

Mr & Mrs S.M. Tyler
Green Acres
17 Bathurst Close
Bath, Avon
BT3 7PY

The Editor
Greenfingers Magazine
44 Old Station Yard
Kingley
Wellington
WT5 7LL

22 May 2002

Dear Sir

Early Hellebores

You may like to know that I followed the advice in last month's edition of your magazine and ordered 26 Hellebores.

When they arrived, they were planted under a fir tree at the bottom of the garden, which you indicated in your article was an ideal spot.

According to your column, the plants would flower profusely from January until late April, and would give my garden much needed colour at this damp and dank time of year.

Unfortunately, I have wasted £35!

Only three of the plants have flowered, and these were a sickly sight. The rest provided a feeble show of leaf and then gave up and dropped all their foliage.

Frost damage was clearly visible on many of the plants and they obviously needed far more light and water.

I am very disappointed at the poor advice I received and have cancelled my subscription to your magazine forthwith.

Yours with regret

S. M. Tyler

2. Increase the left and right page margin by 2 cms

3. Print a copy of the letter.

4. Make sure the document extends just over onto a second page – if necessary, add extra spaces after Yours with regret.

5. Check in Print Preview and then use **Shrink to Fit** to reduce the letter to one page.

6. Reformat Mr Tyler's address, e.g. make it italic and/or apply a different font.

7. Using the ruler, decrease the width of the right margin by approximately 1 cm.

8. Print a copy of the amended letter and save as a new version with the file name Gardening 2.

9. Close the document.

 Module 3, sections 3.3 and 6.1

EXERCISES 12 AND 13

You will need to know how to:

▶ Change to landscape orientation

▶ Move or copy text

Exercise 12 1. Start a new document, select a font size of 14 point and type the following text, centre aligned:

Come to a Party!

2. In a smaller font, type the rest of the invitation and save as Party:

Jane & Rick
Invite .... to their
House Warming
on
Saturday, 22 June
at
12 Rymans Road, Reading

3. Change to landscape orientation and check your document in Print Preview.

4. Close Print Preview and move the line at 12 Rymans Road, Reading so that it appears *above* the date.

5. Increase the font size of House Warming to 16 point and format to italic.

6. Copy House Warming so that the first line of your document reads:

    Come to a House Warming Party!

7. Print a copy of the invitation and save the changes before closing the file.

 Module 3, sections 2.4 and 3.3

Exercise 13 1. Open the file Breakfast.

2. Move grilled kippers so that it appears after cereal.

3. Copy the phrase Breakfast at Hotel Belle Vue so that it also appears at the end of the menu.

4. Now make the following amendments:

    - On the line below cereal, add the following:
      (choice of tomato, orange or pineapple juice)
    - Change fried egg to read: fried, boiled or scrambled egg

5. Delete cereal and replace with stewed prunes.

6. Add an extra course after prunes:
    Porridge, Muesli or Cornflakes

7. Change to landscape orientation and alter the left and right margins and/or spaces between courses so that the menu fits centrally on the page.

8. Update the file to save the changes and print a copy of the amended menu.

 Module 3, sections 2.4 and 3.3

3

EXERCISE 14

You will need to know how to:

- Add numbers and bullet points
- Format number or bullet style
- Insert the date automatically

1. Create the following document:

   THE VERY BEST OF FRANCE

   Normandy: alluring medieval villages, upmarket 19th-century seaside resorts, the island-abbey of Mont St Michael and endless windswept beaches on the Cotentin peninsula.

   Brittany: magnificent beaches lining the north coast, dramatically wind-battered west coast, gentler bays in the south and rolling countryside inland.

   Burgundy: a wealthy region of forests, meadows, magnificent ancient cities and some of the world's great vineyards.

   The Alps: holidays in the mountains, less crowded than the Mediterranean coast, ski lifts to take you up to the peaks for long hikes and après-ski haunts for morning coffee.

2. Add today's date above the heading.

3. Format the place names to bold and underlined.

4. Save the document as **France** and print a copy.

5. Number the paragraphs.

6. In the first paragraph, reorganize the text so that it forms a bulleted list, deleting the final and. It should be set out as follows:

   1. **<u>Normandy</u>:**

      - alluring medieval villages,
      - upmarket 19th-century seaside resorts,
      - the island-abbey of Mont St Michael
      - endless windswept beaches on the Cotentin peninsula.

7. Repeat this formatting for the other three paragraphs.

8. Re-format the bullet points in the final paragraph so that they have a different appearance, e.g. select squares or ticks instead of black circles.

9. Indent the paragraph beginning **The Alps** by 1 cm from the left.

10. Increase the left margin of the page to 4 cm.

11. Save the changes and print a copy of the amended document.

 Module 3, section 3.2

You will need to know how to:

▶ Copy formatting from a selected piece of text

1. Type in the following text:

   Flats

   Living in a flat means plumbing and drainage emergencies can cause problems above and beyond those experienced by house owners. After all, leaking water wherever it comes from won't just cause damage to your own property. It can also cause considerable distress to neighbours and can have potentially disastrous results if you are away for a while.

   However, there are also great advantages to flats. For example, if you are on a fifth floor or above, the views can be fantastic, and burglars are less likely to carry your heavy furniture or electric goods down many flights of stairs or in full view of other residents if they are brazen enough to use the lifts. This makes flats a good choice for those who are away for a good part of their working day.

2. Format the main heading by changing the font type, increasing the font size and making it bold and italic.

3. Fully justify the first paragraph.

4. Double-space the second paragraph and indent it by 1 cm from the right margin.

5. Add the following subheadings to the two paragraphs: *Plumbing* and *Views*

6. Copy the main heading formatting and apply it to the subheadings.

7. Centre the main heading on the page.

8. Save as Flats and print a copy.

9. Now add the following paragraph at the end of the document, keeping the list single spaced:

   Here are some of the emergencies that can happen to flat owners:

   1. Burst pipes
   2. Leaking washing machine
   3. Nail through heating pipe
   4. Blocked kitchen sink
   5. Blocked toilet
   6. Leaking radiator valve

10. Update the file and print a copy.

11. Move the last paragraph so that it becomes the second paragraph under *Plumbing*.

12. Change the numbered list to a bulleted list. Make sure the paragraph justifications are retained and print a final copy before saving and closing.

 Module 3, section 3.1

ADVANCED EXERCISES

EXERCISES 1 AND 2

You will need to know how to:

 ▶ Add headers and footers

 ▶ Create a page break

 ▶ Print selected pages

Exercise 1 1. Open Gardening 2.

2. Start a new page after ... all their foliage.

3. Add Hellebores as a header and your own name and page numbers as a footer.

4. Start a new page after Mr Tyler's signature and enter the following text in italics:

Spring flowers can be the most welcoming as they cheer up dull wintry days. They are often white, pale blue or yellow and contrast well with dark green evergreen leaves. Summer flowers are usually more brightly coloured – oranges, reds and purples – but can fade very quickly.

5. Print a copy of the final (current) page only, and save the file as Gardening 3.

6. Now delete the header and add the word Flowers somewhere in the footer.

7. Save this change and print page 1 of the document only.

8. Close the file.

 Module 3, sections 3.3 and 6.2

Exercise 2   1.   Type out the following text:

Watercolour Painting

The size of a painting is very much a matter of personal preference. There are no rules, but if working small, say 6 x 4in., gives you confidence, that's fine. On the other hand, it can be exciting to work large and it can increase your enthusiasm. If you ever feel you are getting stale or need a change, try working in a different size and you might be amazed at the different work you create.

When painting from nature, the natural arrangement you are confronted with is often the best way to give your work credibility. There are so many different aspects to capture including the temperature, weather, stage of growth and seasonal nature. The same garden in winter, autumn or high summer will look unbelievably different.

2.   Save as Painting and print a copy.

3.   Create a page break after the first paragraph and double space the second paragraph.

4.   Add the following paragraph subheadings: *Size* and *Composition*

5.   Add the following text as a footer: *Exercise on Painting*. Insert the date and page numbers as a header.

6.   Indent the first paragraph 2 cms from the left margin.

7.   Reformat the main heading – apply a different font and underline – and make the document text italic.

8.   Print page 2 only of your document.

9.   Save the changes and close the file.

 Module 3, sections 3.3 and 6.2

EXERCISE 3

You will need to know how to:

▸ Insert special symbols or characters

---

1.   Start a new document and type the following text:

Word processing packages often allow you to use symbols or special characters to liven up your documents. You should be able to find a book, telephone, pair of scissors or smiley face when using Wingdings fonts, or insert symbols for hearts, diamonds, spades and clubs when searching the gallery of Symbols.

2. Save as Symbols.

3. Now add a title – Special Characters – underlined and centred at the top of the page.

4. Start a new paragraph after ... your documents. and insert the following text before You should... :

   A good use for these pictorial symbols is for children's games. For example, if you typed a message in a normal font and then applied Wingdings to the text, it would be impossible to read. Offering the alphabet code for each symbol would then allow a child to decipher the message.

5. For each mention of a special character such as a book or telephone, insert the appropriate symbol into the text – you should find eight. (If you cannot find, e.g. the symbol for clubs (♣), find an alternative and change the text as appropriate.)

6. Indent and double space the second paragraph only.

7. Add a footer showing the date and your name.

8. Save the changes, print a copy and then close the file.

 Module 3, section 2.1

EXERCISE 4

You will need to know how to:

▶ Add page numbers via the **Insert** menu

▶ Save a file into a new folder

---

1. Grimble & Denton, estate agents of 22 Wattis Road, Boscombe, Bournemouth BN5 2AA want to sell a seaside flat. Produce a two-page description of the property (start page 2 with kitchen details), attractively formatted and set out, based on the following information:

   Address of the property: Flat 49, Seaview Road, Southbourne

   Price: £250,000

   Summary: A beautifully appointed ground floor 3-bed property with excellent sea views and balcony, situated close to the picturesque beaches of Southbourne. Included in the price are fitted cupboards, electric hob, carpets and barbecue. There is a garage behind the property which is in a well-kept block built around 1950. Internal inspection highly recommended.

Hall: Carpet, entryphone, radiator.

Sitting room: Large French windows to balcony, seaviews, fireplace, radiator, TV point, telephone point, shelving, Venetian blinds.

Dining Room: Wood floor, radiator, window to rear.

Bedroom 1: Seaviews, fitted cupboards, carpet, radiator.

Bedroom 2: Window to rear, shelves, radiator.

Bedroom 3: Window to side, fitted cupboards, radiator.

Kitchen: Breakfast bar, tiled floor, fitted cupboards, sink unit, electric hob, plumbing for washing machine, door to communal gardens.

Bathroom: Gold taps, shower unit, green suite, glazed window to rear.

2. Add page numbers using the **Insert** menu.

3. When saving the file, first click the **Create New Folder** button in the **Save As** dialog box to create a folder labelled Bournemouth, and save the file into this folder with the file name Property.

4. Close the file and close your word processing application.

5. Reopen Property (you may first have to locate and open the Bournemouth folder) and make the following amendments: Bedroom 2 has no shelves; the kitchen has a wall-mounted electric oven; and there is also a Study with a glass chandelier and wooden floor.

6. Save the amendments and print one copy before closing the file.

 Module 3, section 3.3

EXERCISES 5 AND 6

You will need to know how to:

▶ Insert Clip Art

▶ Amend Clip Art, e.g. resize, crop or border

▶ Delete Clip Art

Exercise 5 1. Open Property, click below the estate agent's address and insert an appropriate picture from the Clip Art Gallery.

2. Resize the picture and align it centrally on the page.

3. Amend the picture, e.g. by adding a background colour and border, cropping one area and increasing the contrast.

4. Print page 1 of the document displaying the picture.

5. Insert a text box in a space at the end of the property details.

6. Return to the gallery and find and insert a different image into the text box. If necessary, resize the picture inside the box.

7. Drag the box so that the picture is positioned on the right of the page, and add colours and borders.

8. Add today's date as a footer.

9. Update the file and print a copy of the last page only.

10. Close the file.

 Module 3, section 4.2

Exercise 6
1. Start a new document. Enter the words: Welcome to Boscombe Zoo on one line and Open every day except Christmas Day a few lines below.

2. Centre the text and make the heading italic, font size 24 point.

3. Save the file as Zoo into the Bournemouth folder.

4. In the space between the two lines of text, insert a picture of an animal from the Clip Art Gallery.

5. Centre and enlarge the picture so that it fills about a quarter of the page – check in Print Preview. Make sure the sentence beginning Open every day ... remains below the picture.

6. Add a thick, coloured border to the picture via the **Format** menu.

7. Add the following bulleted list below the picture, indented by 5 cms from the left margin and formatted attractively, e.g. bold, font size 16 or 18 point:

● Circus spectacular show twice a day
● See the animals being fed
● Cuddle baby lambs and goats
● Restaurant and cafe open all day
● Take a train ride round the zoo

8. Print a copy of the poster, first adjusting the picture size if necessary to make sure you only print on one page.

9. Now delete the picture and insert an alternative that can be on either an animal or circus theme but must be positioned *below* the bulleted list. Use the cropping tool to cut off any unwanted edges and add a coloured background.

10. Format the bullets to a different style.

11. Print a copy of the amended document.

12. Update and close the file.

 Module 3, section 4.2

You will need to know how to:

◆ Change case

◆ Apply hanging indents

1. Start a new document and type the following text:

STANLEY ROAD HOSPITAL TRUST

The following opportunity has arisen for a clear-thinking, caring individual to join our acclaimed Trust as a full-time ASSISTANT. You will help trained nurses assess need and deliver care to the many older patients at our brand new SALTWOOD ANNEXE.

For the post, we are looking for an exceptional person. You must have first-aid training, good communication skills, be patient and caring and enjoy working flexibly.

To apply, please send us a full c.v. together with the names of two referees.

For further information, write to Marion Hobbs, Saltwood Annexe, Webleton Hospital, Grundy Close, Chesterham. Or phone her on 0166778 2349.

2. Print a copy and save as Hospital.

3. Using change case facilities, make the following amendments:

   a) change the heading to title case (i.e. Stanley Road Hospital Trust).

   b) change c.v. to C.V.

   c) change ASSISTANT to lower case

   d) change SALTWOOD ANNEXE to title case (i.e. Saltwood Annexe)

4. Move the second sentence, beginning 'You will help trained nurses ...' so that it becomes the second sentence in the second paragraph. Ensure there are no extra spaces.

5. Centre align the heading.

6. Apply hanging indents to all the paragraphs.

7. Update the file and print a copy before closing.

 Module 3, sections 3.1 and 3.2

EXERCISE 8

You will need to know how to:

▶ Add borders and shading

1. Create the following document, proof-read it and save as **Advert**.

   SEE-RIGHT-THRU DOUBLE GLAZING

   Who can you trust to install double glazing?

   Few people are experts in double glazing, So if you're looking to improve your home with PVC-U windows, doors or a conservatory – and don't fancy entrusting such a major decision to a possible cowboy – use us.

   One call and you will be in touch with a nationwide network of approved, fully trained installers who are monitored regularly by a team of inspectors.

   We use only the best materials, and there's a free 20-year guarantee.

   Call now on Freephone 0800 444555 for a no-strings quotation.

   SEE-RIGHT-THRU

   The name to trust

2. Centre the text, then increase the font size for the heading and make it bold.

3. Delete the word us at the end of the second paragraph and replace with SEE-RIGHT-THRU copied from the end of the document.

4. Apply a thick, coloured border to the heading and check that it extends across the width of the page.

5. Apply shading to the heading background.

6. Box the last paragraph so that only the text is bordered.

7. Insert an appropriate picture from the Clip Art Gallery (e.g. windows, houses, etc.) just below the heading and centre it on the page.

8. Replace each mention of THRU with THROUGH using the **Edit | Replace** menu.

9. After the sentence ending ... **guarantee**, insert the following numbered paragraph left aligned:

   1. We are fast
   2. We are careful
   3. We leave the site tidy
   4. We are the best.

10. Move the paragraph beginning **One call** ... so that it follows the free-phone number.

11. Print a copy and close the file, making sure you save the changes.

 Module 3, section 3.2

3

EXERCISE 9

You will need to know how to:

▶ Create tables

▶ Edit tables

1. Start a new document and type the title: Landscombe College Evening Classes.

2. Insert the following table, ensuring all columns are wide enough to display entries on a single line and row heights are at least 0.6 cm:

Title	Day	Tutor	Time	Room
Bee-keeping	Monday	Jamie Green	7–9 p.m.	B3
Yoga for Beginners	Tuesday	Pat Hurt	6.30–8.00 p.m.	Hall
Calligraphy	Monday	Serena Holden	10–12 a.m.	C14
Car Mechanics	Wednesday	Jack Byrne	6–8 p.m.	Workshop
Watercolour painting	Tuesday	Nancy Smythe	2–4 p.m.	B9

3. Save as **Classes** into a new folder named **College** and print a copy.

4. Add two new classes after 'Yoga':

- Computing for Beginners on Thursday, at 3–5 p.m., in Room C14, tutor Howard Maynard
- Advanced Yoga on Wednesday, at 7–9 p.m., in the Hall, tutor Pat Hurt.

5. Delete the Calligraphy course record, making sure you don't leave empty cells.

6. Centre align all headings except Title and format the text so that it stands out, e.g. use bold and/or increase font size.

7. Apply different borders and shading formats to the table.

8. Save the changes and print a copy.

9. On a line below the table, type the following sentence:

New students may like to know that the following videos acquired by the College are relevant to this term's classes and may be available for hire.

10. Create and format a new 5 × 5 table containing the following data:

Title: Yoga For All
Presenter: The Graceful Goddess
Hire charge: £1.50
Length: 110 mins
Available: On loan

Title: Bees For Life
Presenter: William and Sarah Price
Hire charge: £2.50
Length: 150 mins
Available: Yes

Title: Know Your Car
Presenter: Ray B. Wise
Hire charge: £3.00
Length: 90 mins
Available: Yes

Title: Keeping Bees
Presenter: Walter Mitts
Hire charge: £1.50
Length: 90 mins
Available: On loan

11. Add your name as a header, right-aligned, then update the file and print a copy before closing.

 Module 3, section 4.1

EXERCISE 10

You will need to know how to:

♦ Apply AutoFormats to tables

1. Create a table of six items such as books, records, films, etc., and classify them under at least five headings, e.g. author, title, price, category and publication date. Make sure all data is fully displayed.

2. Save with a suitable file name and print a copy.

3. Delete the second record, making sure you don't leave any empty cells.

4. Add a further item as record number 5.

5. Choose an AutoFormat and apply it to the table.

6. Move the table so that it is centred on the page.

7. Increase the font size for the category headings and make all data entries italic.

8. Add a footer to include the text **My Table**, the date and the exercise number.

9. Format the exercise details in the footer to bold and underline the date.

10. Update and print a copy before closing the file.

 Module 3, section 4.1

EXERCISES 11 AND 12

You will need to know how to:

♦ Use and set tabs (→)

♦ Move the position of tabs

♦ Apply a font colour

Exercise 11 1. Enter the following column headings across the page:

Make   Type   Price   Colour

2. Set out the following information using tabs (→). Use decimal tabs for Price and left or centre tabs for the other details. Set the **Type** column at 4 cm and the **Price** column at 8 cm.

Miele → oven → £153.99 → black
Electrolux → fridge-freezer → £245 → white
Tricity → cooker hood → £76.99 → silver
Servis → dishwasher → £196.50 → brown
Philips → washing machine → £279.99 → white

2. Save the file as Household items and print a copy.

3. Format the column headings to blue, underlined.

4. Add the following item:

   Hoover → upright vacuum cleaner → £89 → red

   Move the Price column to the right (and/or Type column to the left) to ensure all details will be fully displayed.

5. Save and print an updated copy. Close the file.

 Module 3, sections 3.1 and 3.2

Exercise 12 1. Enter the following data using tabs. Set centre tabs for Surname, decimal tabs for Per cent and right tabs for the numerical data.

CLASS MARKS 2000

First Name	Surname	Maths	Science	English	Per cent	Total
Janet	Brown-Smythe	40	35	38	75.33	113
Peter	Smith	23	38	46	71.33	107
Richard	Wellington	31	48	40	79.33	119
Harry	Longbottom	15	23	37	50.00	75
John	Baker	38	26	22	57.33	86
Mary	French	50	50	50	100.00	150

2. Save as Marks and print a copy.

3. Format the headings to italic, the names to bold and the numerical data to red.

4. Add the following student details below the entry for Richard Wellington, making sure the columns are adjusted to display the data fully:

   Danielle-Celeste Courvoisier, Maths 23, Science 44, English 19, 57.33 per cent and a Total of 86.

5. Update the file and print a copy before closing.

 Module 3, sections 3.1 and 3.2

You will need to know how to:

▶ Apply styles and use templates

1. Type in the following company name and centre it on the page: Home Decorating Ltd.

2. Below this, type the following memo:

   To: Denise Watermill, Marketing Manager
   From: Arnold Morton, Ceramics Department
   Copied to: Head of Purchasing
   Subject: Bali and Hong Kong
   Date: (today's)

   With regard to the recent sales, I am writing to let you know that there was a huge demand for the new lines we purchased from Bali and Hong Kong. Many customers asked when we would be stocking smaller items such as soup bowls, spoons and tea cups, and I feel such items would almost walk off the shelves if we had them in stock.

   I suggest we have a meeting as soon as is practicable to discuss purchasing more items from the Far East, and a possible television advertising campaign to accompany these new goods.

3. Save as Ceramics and print a copy.

4. Now apply the following formatting: Heading 1 style to the company name; Heading 2 style to the subject of the memo; a lower level heading style to the date and people's names and job titles; and a body text style to the main text.

5. Update the file and print a copy.

6. Copy the main text of Ceramics into the clipboard and then select a memo template from those available, in order to create a different version of the memo.

7. Paste in the main text and type in the names, job titles and company name.

8. Format the text as you like and save as Ceramics 2.

9. Print a copy and then save and close both memos.

 Module 3, sections 3.1 and 3.3

You will need to know how to:

◗ Create a data source

◗ Carry out a Mail Merge

Exercise 14 1. In a new document, type the heading Wilmington College, Derbyshire, apply italics and bold format, and centre it on the page. Now use this document as the basis for a mail merge.

2. Set up the following data source containing only the fieldnames shown, save as **Staff** and enter all the records:

Firstname	Surname	Department	Food
Marion	Peters	Business	crisps
David	Holmes	IT	pizza
Ken	Jackman	Business	salad
Mel	Griffiths	English	quiche
Beverley	Garland	IT	jelly

3. Type the following memo, inserting field names as shown:

To: <<Firstname>> <<Surname>>,<<Department>> Department
From: (your name)
Date: (today's)
Subject: End of Year Party

As spokesperson for the course, I am writing to ask you to come to our final session in the Staff Room on Friday at 2.00 p.m. We would like to hold a party as a fun way to end the course, and would like you to bring some <<Food>> as a small contribution.

Please let me know if you are unable to attend.

4. Check that all records have been merged.

5. Print a copy of the document displaying field names.

6. Merge to a new document and print three memos displaying data taken from the database.

7. Save and close the data source and main document files.

 Module 3, section 5.1

Exercise 15 1. Start a new document and then create the following data source to use for a mail merge. Save as **Names** and enter all the records.

Title	Firstname	Surname	Town	Age	Allowance
Mr	James	Smith	York	62	£2,400
Mr	Paul	Black	Leicester	64	£3,580
Mrs	Jean	Kenton	York	72	£4,000
Mr	Harry	Oldham	Birmingham	62	£2,400
Mr	Peter	Witton	York	69	£3,765
Ms	Sarah	Danby	Leicester	66	£3,245
Mr	Harry	Smith	Manchester	69	£3,765
Miss	Sally	Black	Birmingham	77	£5,490

2. Create and edit the following main document, inserting appropriate field names as shown.

<<Title>> <<Firstname>> <<Surname>>
<<Town>>

Date: (today's)

Dear <<Title>> <<Surname>>

Extra payment

As a resident of <<Town>> who has reached the age of <<Age>> and who has been living in the city for 2 years, we have the power to pay you an extra <<Allowance>>.

This will be sent in the form of a cheque to your home address at the end of the month.

Yours sincerely

Gordon Best

On behalf of the Inland Revenue

3. Print a copy of the main document showing the field names.

4. Now print two copies of the document displaying details taken from two different records.

5. Save the main document as **Payments** and update the data source before closing both files.

 Module 3, section 5.1

Spreadsheets

This module tests your knowledge of spreadsheets and charts. In the ECDL exam you will need to know how to set up a spreadsheet, format numbers and text and use formulae to perform a range of calculations. There are also exercises in this module on sorting data, functions such as Average and Sum, and creating and amending different styles of chart.

Subjects covered in this section:

Introductory exercises		ECDL module
1–2	Entering and editing data; changing column widths; simple calculations; saving and printing a spreadsheet	**4.1.1, 4.2.1, 4.2.3, 4.4.1 and 4.7.3**
3–5	Formatting data and cells; using SUM and AutoSum	**4.4.3, 4.5.1 and 4.5.2**
6–8	Copying cells and data; inserting and deleting columns and rows	**4.2.3 and 4.2.5**
9–11	Adding borders and shading; changing page orientation; printing spreadsheets	**4.5.3 and 4.7.1**
12–14	Using absolute cell references and applying AutoFormats	**4.4.2 and 4.5.2**

Advanced exercises		ECDL module
1–3	Adding headers and footers; centre-aligning headings; using the AVERAGE function	**4.4.3, 4.5.3 and 4.7.1**
4	Modifying margins; using **Edit	Replace**	**4.2.6 and 4.7.1**
5–6	Creating a database and sorting records	**4.2.7**
7–8	Creating, editing and printing a chart	**4.6.1 and 4.7.3**
9–12	Formatting chart elements; changing a chart type; selecting non-adjacent cell ranges	**4.2.2 and 4.6.1**
13–14	Copying spreadsheets and charts; renaming worksheets	**4.2.5, 4.3.1 and 4.6.1**
15	Using the IF function; wrapping text; applying font colour	**4.4.3 and 4.5.2**

You will need to know how to:

- Enter text and numerical data
- Amend cell entries
- Widen columns
- Perform simple calculations
- Save and print a spreadsheet

Exercise 1 1. Create the following spreadsheet:

	A	B	C	D	E
1	DARTS				
2	Name	Score 1	Score 2	Score 3	Final score
3	Marion	8	11	3	
4	Harry	12	22	6	
5	Steve	3	5	18	
6	David	18	16	5	
7	Joan	9	12	11	

2. Enter a simple formula in cell *E3* to work out **Marion's** final score (*i.e. Score 1 + Score 2 + Score 3*).

3. Calculate final scores for all the other darts players.

4. Save the file as **Darts** and print one copy.

5. On a new row, add the name **Elizabeth-Jane** and scores of **11, 15** and **20**.

6. Widen column *A* to display all names fully.

7. Calculate **Elizabeth-Jane's** final score in *E8*.

8. Change **Steve's** Score 2 to **9** and check that his final score is updated automatically.

9. Change **Marion's** name to **Marigold**.

10. Print a copy of the revised spreadsheet and then update and close the file.

 Module 4, sections 1.1, 2.1, 2.3, 4.1 and 7.3

Exercise 2 **1.** Start a new workbook and create the following spreadsheet:

	A	B	C	D
1	SHOPPING			
2	Item	Cost (£)	Number	Final price (£)
3	Catfood	0.4	10	
4	Milk	0.38	4	
5	Loaf	0.87	2	
6	Marmalade	1.15	1	
7	Pasta	0.56	3	
8	Pineapple	1.3	2	
9	Lemonade	0.89	3	

2. Enter a formula in *D3* to calculate the final price of Catfood (i.e. *Cost ×
   Number*).

3. Work out the final price for all other items.

4. Save the file as **Shopping** and print one copy.

5. Now amend the entry in cell *C2* to read **Number Bought**, and widen
   columns *C* and *D* to display the full entries.

6. Make the following changes: **Pasta** costs **49p**; replace **Pineapple** with
   Melon; and increase the number of pints of **Milk** bought to **6**.

7. Check that the final prices are updated automatically and print a copy of
   the amended spreadsheet.

8. Save and close the file.

 Module 4, sections 1.1, 2.1, 2.3, 4.1 and 7.3

EXERCISES 3, 4 AND 5

You will need to know how to:

- Format text and numerical data

- Align cell contents

- Calculate totals using the SUM function or AutoSum

- Open a previously saved spreadsheet

Exercise 3   1.   Reopen Shopping and right-align all column headings except Item.

2.   Type Total in cell *A10* and enter a formula in *D10* to work out the overall total for the shopping bill.

3.   Format data entries in the Cost and Final price columns to currency.

4.   Change the title in *A1* to SHOPPING AT SUPERMART and increase the font size to 14 point.

5.   Print a copy of the amended spreadsheet.

6.   Now make the following changes: Marmalade costs £1.35 and a loaf is 93p. Check that the total is updated automatically before saving and closing the file.

7.   Open Darts and format all the scores to display two decimal places.

8.   Right-align all column headings except Name.

9.   Format the players' names to bold.

10.   Select all the entries on the spreadsheet and apply a different font.

11.   Save as Dart2 and print a copy before closing the file.

 Module 4, sections 4.3, 5.1 and 5.2

Exercise 4   1.   Create the following spreadsheet, ensuring all data is fully displayed:

Shares					
Months	Bellings	Thatchers	Gordington	Lowden	Witneys
Jan	2.4	12.6	22	0.5	18
Feb	3.7	13.2	14.6	0.96	16.5
Mar	1.6	7.9	18	1.3	17
Apr	0.75	5.6	30.3	4.1	17.8
May	4.9	14.1	31.7	3.7	16.4
Total					
Average					

2.   Calculate the total for Bellings' shares.

3.   Calculate totals for all other shares and save the file as Shares.

4.   Format all numerical entries to currency and two decimal places.

5.   Calculate the average price of Bellings' shares (i.e. *Total/Number of months*).

6.   Work out all other averages and format the Average row as currency to one decimal place.

7. Format the title to bold and the column headings to italic.

8. Centre the column headings.

9. Save the changes and print a copy.

10. Now make the following amendments: Thatchers' share price in April was £6.40 and Gordington's in January was £24. The name Witneys should be changed to Morgan.

11. Update the file and print a copy of the amended spreadsheet before closing.

 Module 4, sections 4.3, 5.1 and 5.2

Exercise 5
1. You and a friend had the following meal:

   Melon (you) £1.25
   Soup (friend) £1.00
   Steak & kidney pie (both) £4.50 a portion
   Chips (you) 80p
   Jacket potato (friend) 75p
   Salad (both) £1.25 each
   Ice-cream (you) £1.10
   Apple pie (friend) £2.10
   Coffee (both) 85p per cup

2. Set up a spreadsheet with the title **Restaurant** to show both your meals: type your names in cells *B2* and *C2* and enter all the food items in column A. Make sure cells contain only numerical data (i.e. no 'p' for 'pence'). Leave cells blank if you did not have a particular item.

3. Widen columns to display the full entries, format prices to currency and right-align your names.

4. Add a row labelled **TOTAL** and enter formulae to calculate both bills.

5. Apply bold format to the name of the person with the more expensive meal.

6. Save as **Restaurant** and print a copy of the spreadsheet.

7. Close the file.

8. Reopen **Restaurant** and make the following changes: ice-cream cost 95p; you had two cups of **coffee**; and your friend had **fruit salad** at 90p instead of **apple pie**.

9. Did the same person have the most expensive meal this time? If not, change the name in bold.

10. Update the file and print a copy of the amended spreadsheet before closing.

 Module 4, sections 4.3, 5.1 and 5.2

You will need to know how to:

- ◆ Copy cell entries and date series
- ◆ Insert or delete columns and rows

Exercise 6 1. Create the following spreadsheet:

Own Brand Cereal Prices					
SHOP	Gateway	Waitrose	Tesco	Co-op	Safeway
Size of pack (gm)	500	750	450	1000	1500
Price per pack	2.5	2.8	2	4.5	3.75
Cost per 100 gm					

2. Work out the cost of 100 gm **Gateway** cereal using the formula *Price/Size × 100*.

3. Copy this formula along the row to work out the cost of 100 gm of all the other cereals.

4. Format the shop names to italic and right-align.

5. Print a copy of the spreadsheet and save as **Cereal**.

6. Now insert a new column to the right of **Tesco** and add the following details:

   Asda, 1000gm pack costs £3.50.

7. Copy across the formula to calculate the cost of 100 gm of **Asda cereal**.

8. Delete the column containing the entry for **Waitrose**.

9. Insert a new row below the title and type: **Comparison**

10. Format the prices to currency.

11. Increase the title font size and apply bold format.

12. Save and print the amended spreadsheet before closing the file.

 Module 4, sections 2.3 and 2.5

Exercise 7 1. Create the following spreadsheet:

Dates	Postage	Coffee/Tea	Cleaning	Stationery
January	13.5	11	14	15.75
	7.65	2.5	14	17.38
	19.38	3.45	14	20.75
	9.23	4.15	17	9.5
	11.68	2.17	17	12.45

2. Insert a new row 1 and type the heading: PETTY CASH EXPENSES.

3. Copy the date series down the first column.

4. Add a new row **Totals** and enter a formula to calculate total postage costs. Copy this formula across the row to produce totals for the other items.

5. Adjust column widths and format the column headings to bold, font size 14. Format all numerical data to currency.

6. Save as **Office** and print a copy.

7. Now insert a new column after **Cleaning** headed **Furniture** and enter £385 for **March** and £37.99 for **May**. Calculate the total for **Furniture**.

8. Make the following changes:

    ● cleaning in **April** is now £14;
    ● coffee costs £3.50 in **February**;
    ● the **Stationery** heading should now read **Stationery/Disks**.

9. Update the file and print the amended spreadsheet before closing.

 Module 4, sections 2.3 and 2.5

Exercise 8 1. Create the following spreadsheet and save as Bookings. Reformat the Price column if it displays dates. Widen columns to ensure all data is fully displayed and print a copy.

Holiday Bookings					
Date of Booking	Surname	Villa	Start date	End date	Price
02-Feb	Billings	Caprice	01-Jun	08-Jun	209
25-Feb	Derbyshire	Miramar	15-Jun	22-Jun	354
03-Mar	Winslow	Capri	25-May	1-Jun	567
15-Mar	Harris	Nuit	15-Jun	22-Jun	248
07-Apr	Davis	Miramar	20-Jul	27-Jul	422
16-Apr	Pentford	Soleil	18-May	25-Jun	680

2. Right-align all headings except Date of Booking and format to bold. Left align data in the Date of Booking column.

3. Format all prices to currency, to display the £ symbol and no decimal places.

4. Apply a different date format to all dates, e.g. 02-Feb becomes 2/2/02.

5. Add a new row heading: Total and work out the total income for the holiday bookings.

6. Insert a new column between End date and Price headed Max. number and use the following table to enter the correct figures:

Villa	Max. number
Caprice	5
Miramar	4
Capri	6
Nuit	3
Soleil	4

7. Head a new column Price per person and enter a formula to work this out for the first booking (*Price/Max. number*). Copy the formula down the column to find the price per person for all bookings.

8. Format the Price per person column to currency and two decimal places.

9. Make the following amendments: Billings should read Browning; the price for Nuit should be £295; delete the Davis booking completely, leaving no empty cells.

10. Copy the title **Holiday Bookings** to a new row underneath the spreadsheet data and format it to bold.

11. Realign any entries to neaten the spreadsheet appearance.

12. Update and print a copy of the amended spreadsheet before closing the file.

 Module 4, sections 2.3 and 2.5

EXERCISES 9, 10 AND 11

You will need to know how to:

◗ Add borders and shading

◗ Change page orientation

◗ Print to fit one page

Exercise 9 1. Create a spreadsheet to show the following recipe details:

Pizza			
Item	Quantity for 2	Cost per item	Final Price for 2
Strong flour (lb)	1.5	0.70	
Yeast (sachet)	1	0.20	
Fat (oz)	2	0.40	
Olive oil (tbs)	3	0.30	
Tomatoes	2	0.25	
Mozzarella (oz)	6	0.80	
Spicy sausage (oz)	4	0.85	
Onion	1	0.30	
Total			

2. Enter a formula to calculate the final price of **strong flour** and copy this formula down the column.

3. Enter a formula to add together the entries in the final price column to find the overall cost.

4. Right-align all column headings except Item.

5. Format quantities to two decimal places, and all prices to currency.

6. Add a border and shade the background of the column headings. Then shade the Item column entries a different colour.

7. Save as Pizza and print a copy.

8. Insert a new column between Quantity for 2 and Cost headed Quantity for 30. Enter a formula to work out the quantity of flour needed to make pizza for 30 (i.e. *Quantity for 2 × 15*). Copy this formula down the column and format to two decimal places.

9. Change to landscape orientation.

10. Type your name in *L2* (or the cell after the dotted lines indicating the edge of page 1) and check in Print Preview that your name is on page 2.

11. Go to **Page Setup** and select the option to **Fit to 1 page**. Now check in Print Preview that your name is visible alongside the spreadsheet data.

12. Print a copy of the amended spreadsheet.

13. Save and close the file.

 Module 4 sections 5.3 and 7.1

Exercise 10 1. Create the following spreadsheet with the title *TVs* and save the Workbook with the same name.

Make	Price	Size of screen (ins)	Features
Westwood	159.99	20	Stereo
Jacksons	198.75	14	Televideo
Merit	229.99	14	DVD-player
Piccolo	99.99	14	Silver
Bradleys	179	17	Silver
Clerical	79.99	2.3	Pocket-size

2. Format the prices to currency and two decimal places.

3. Right-align all headings except Make and format all headings to bold.

4. On a new row, type the row heading Total and enter a formula to work out the total cost of all the TVs.

5. On a row below that, headed **Average**, enter a formula to work out the average price (Total/6).

6. Save and print a copy of the spreadsheet.

7. Now insert a new column headed: **Teletext** between **Screen** and **Features** and enter **Yes** for all TVs except the **Clerical**.

8. Add a further column headed: **No. in stock** and enter the following data:

Westwood	20
Jacksons	14
Merit	2
Piccolo	12
Bradleys	5
Clerical	8

9. Make any further changes necessary to width of columns or alignment and add different borders and shading to improve the attractiveness of the spreadsheet.

10. Check the spreadsheet in print preview and change to landscape orientation.

11. Print a copy of the spreadsheet, making sure it prints on one page.

12. Save and close the file.

 Module 4 sections 5.3 and 7.1

Exercise 11 1. Create the following spreadsheet and save as Writing:

Writer's Costs				
MONTH	PENS	PAPER	DISKS	COFFEE
JAN	2.5	3.7	1.8	0.65
FEB	3.67	9.5	3.5	2.4
MAR	1.8	2.7	4.85	2.5
APR	5.5	0	2.7	0.9
MAY	2	3.45	1.1	2.45

2. Right-align all column headings except MONTH.

3. Add a new column headed *TOTAL* and enter a formula to calculate the total costs in January. Copy this formula down the column to find the total for other months.

4. Insert a new column after *PAPER* and before *DISKS* headed *TRAVEL*. Enter the following data:

    Jan: 15.34, Feb: 7.78, Mar: 12.9, Apr 22.5, May 5

5. Check that the *TOTAL* column now includes travel costs.

6. Work out and enter the Overall Total at the bottom of the TOTAL column and add this text as a row heading in column *A*.

7. Work out the average expenditure per month and display this figure under the overall total. Use the formula *OVERALL TOTAL divided by 5* (i.e. the number of months) and enter Average as a row heading.

8. Display the expenditure figures as currency to two decimal places.

9. Display the *TOTAL* column figures in Integer format (i.e. whole numbers).

10. Apply borders and shading to enhance the appearance of the data.

11. Landscape page orientation and print a copy of the spreadsheet, fitting it on one page.

12. Save and close the file.

 Module 4 sections 5.3 and 7.1

You will need to know how to:

▶ Use absolute cell references

▶ Apply AutoFormats

Exercise 12 1. Create the following spreadsheet and save as Meal.

	A	B	C
1	Food	Price(£)	Discount offered
2	Omelette	4.50	
3	Salad	2.00	
4	Chips	1.50	
5	Fudge cake	2.75	
6	Tea	0.85	
7	Total		
8	Final Price		
9	Discount is:		
10	5%		
11			

2. Enter a formula in *B7* to calculate the total food bill.

3. Enter a formula in *C2* to calculate the discount offered on **Omelette** (i.e. Price × Discount). Use the cell address *A10* in the formula, *not* the actual figure 5%.

4. Copy the formula down column *C* to work out the discount on other meal items without first making *A10* absolute. What do you think the formula will look like in cell *C3*? (The result will look wrong because the formula will include a reference to cell *A11* that has nothing in it.)

5. Return to cell *C2* and absolute *A10* in the formula, i.e. it will become A10. Now copy the amended formula down the column to replace the original entries. All discounts should now look correct.

6. Calculate the total **Discount offered** in *C7*.

7. Enter a formula in *B8* to work out the final price for the meal (i.e. *Price Total – Discount offered Total*).

8. Reformat the spreadsheet to show currency and apply your preferred AutoFormat. Save and print a copy.

9. Change the discount shown in *A10* to (a) 10% and (b) 17.5%. Check that the final prices change and print the two new versions.

 Module 4 sections 4.2 and 5.2

Exercise 13 1. Open a new workbook and on the first line enter the title **Sale of Tiles for January**. On the row below the title enter the following column headings:

Code number Colour Price of pack Cost of 1 tile Packs sold Final price

Adjust the column widths to display the full entries.

2. All column headings except **Code number** should be right-aligned.

3. Enter the following data (to retain a '0' at the start of each Code number, either format column *A* to text first, or press ' before typing the first '0'):

	A	B	C	D	E	F
1	Sale of Tiles for January					
2	Code number	Colour	Price of pack	Cost of 1 tile	Packs sold	Final price
3	005	Red	6.5		20	
4	041	Blue	8.75		35	
5	018	Green	4.95		30	
6	019	Green	18.45		10	
7	049	Blue	33.5		5	
8	006	Brown	3.25		25	
9	TOTAL					
10	No. tiles per pack	25				

4. Save the file as **Tiles** and print a copy of the spreadsheet.

5. Enter a formula to calculate the **Final price** of packs of **Red** tiles sold that month (i.e. *Price of pack* × *Packs sold*). Copy this formula down the column to find the final price for all other tiles sold.

6. The Tile Company decide that **Blue** tiles coded **049** should be listed in a different category. Delete the complete entry for these tiles.

7. Now make the following amendments: the price of packs of **Green** tiles, code 018 is £7.95 and the colour of tile 041 is **Black**.

8. The **Brown** tiles should have been entered as **Patterned–Brown**. Amend the entry and widen the **Colour** column to display this name in full.

9. Calculate the cost of one red tile (i.e. Price of pack/No. tiles per pack) using the cell address and *not* the figure 25 in the formula. Copy this formula to find the cost of each type of tile sold and format the entries to currency.

10. Calculate the total number of packs sold and the total of the **Final price** column.

11. Save these changes.

12. On a row below the **Red** tile entry, insert a new row and add the following details: **Yellow** tiles, code number 026, each pack costs £12.45 and the number of packs sold is 14. Complete all entries for these tiles making sure all totals are updated.

13. Reformat all remaining prices to currency and apply an AutoFormat to improve the appearance of the spreadsheet.

14. Change the number of tiles per pack shown in *B10* to 50. Check the new cost of each tile and border the row of the *cheapest* tile to make it stand out.

15. Print a copy of the amended spreadsheet before saving the changes and closing the file.

 Module 4 sections 4.2 and 5.2

Exercise 14 You need to buy new carpets for a sitting room, bedroom and bathroom, so create the following spreadsheet to help you work out the cost.

1. Name and save the spreadsheet as **New Carpets** and enter the following column headings:

    Room Length (ft) Width (ft) Area (sq ft) Area (sq metres) Cost (sq metres)

2. Enter the following measurements:

Room	Length (ft)	Width (ft)
Sitting	14	10.5
Bed	9	8.25
Bath	6	7

3. Enter a formula to work out the area of the sitting room carpet in sq ft (i.e. *Length* × *Width*) and then copy this formula down the column to work out the areas for the other carpets.

4. Print a copy of the spreadsheet.

5. One sq ft is equivalent to 0.0929 sq metres. Type this figure into cell *A9*.

6. Enter a formula to convert the area of the sitting room carpet from sq ft to sq metres (i.e. multiply it by 0.0929) using the cell address *A9* in the formula and *not* the actual figure. Copy this formula down the column to work out the areas of the bedroom and bathroom carpets in sq metres.

7. The sitting room carpet costs £22.85 per sq metre, the bedroom carpet costs £19.25 per sq metre and the bathroom carpet costs £8 per sq metre. Enter these prices into the **Cost** column.

8. Now head a new column **Final Price** and enter a formula to work this out for the sitting room carpet, i.e. *Cost per sq metre* × *Area per sq metre*. Copy this figure down the column to work out the final price for all three carpets.

9. Add a new row headed **Total** and total the cost of carpets in the **Final Price** column.

10. Format the **Cost** and **Final Price** columns to currency and all other numerical data to two decimal places. Right-align all column headings except **Room** and apply your own choice of borders or shading.

11. Update the spreadsheet and print a copy that fits one page before closing the file.

 Module 4 sections 4.2 and 5.2

ADVANCED EXERCISES

EXERCISES 1, 2 AND 3

You will need to know how to:

- Add headers and footers

- Centre headings across the width of a spreadsheet

- Use the AVERAGE function

Exercise 1 1. Set up the following spreadsheet showing the distribution of money to various charities over six months.

	A	B	C	D	E	F	G	H	I
1	Charity Contributions								
2									
3	Charity	Percent	Jan	Feb	March	April	May	June	Average
4	RNIB	50%	1000	1840	645	2500	2340	1158	
5	Birds	12%	240	442	155	600	562		
6	Lifeboats	5%	100	184	64		234	116	
7	Sue Ryder	25%	500	920	322	1250	1170	579	
8	Oxfam	8%		294	103	400	374	185	
9	Total		2000			5000		2315	

2. Enter a formula in *B9* to check that the percentages add up to 100.

3. Enter appropriate formulae to work out the missing **January, April** and **June** entries (i.e. *Percent × Total*) and **February, March** and **May** totals.

4. Use the **AVERAGE** function to display average contributions to the various charities.

5. Add formatting, a border and some shading to improve the attractiveness of the spreadsheet, and realign entries as necessary.

6. Format contributions to currency with no decimal places.

7. Centre the heading **Charity Contributions** across the width of the spreadsheet.

8. Add *DISTRIBUTION OF MONEY* as a header and your name and the date as a footer, and then save and print a copy before closing the file.

 Module 4 sections 4.3, 5.3 and 7.1

Exercise 2 1. Create a spreadsheet to show your expenditure over four months. Your income is £200 per month, but in the second month you earned an extra £45.

Your outgoings were as follows:

	1st month	2nd month	3rd month	4th month
Heating	£25	£25	£25	£25
Food	£75	£30	£60	£45
Travel	£5	£12.50	£5	£2.50
Entertainment	0	£15.50	£5	0
Clothes	£65	£13.45	£48	£7

2. Format the spreadsheet attractively and add borders and shading. Save as Expenditure.

3. Insert a new row 1 and type the heading:

Expenditure over four months

Centre it across the width of the spreadsheet.

4. Add your name and the date as a header and *Exercise 16* as a footer.

5. Add rows as necessary to show your total expenditure each month, your income and what was left over.

6. In a new column headed **Average**, work out the average amount you spent in each category.

7. Save and print the spreadsheet.

8. Insert an extra row for **Newspapers & Magazines** below Travel: you spent 75p each month. Check that the totals take this row into account and that all entries are fully displayed.

9. Delete the entire row showing **Entertainment** expenditure and then insert an extra row above **Heating** labelled **Holidays**. Enter £350 for the third month only and make sure the totals have been updated.

10. Save the changes and print a copy showing the new totals.

 Module 4 sections 4.3, 5.3 and 7.1

Exercise 3　1.　Create a spreadsheet to show the average temperature in different locations, using the following data:

Temperature °C	Jan	Feb	Mar	Apr	May	Jun
Brize Norton	4.3	3.7	6.3	7.9	11.4	14.4
Oxford	3.7	4.2	5.8	8.4	11.7	14.9
Cambridge	3.4	3.9	5.7	8.3	11.6	14.7
Sheffield	3.8	3.9	5.4	7.8	10.9	14.1
Durham	2.8	3.2	4.6	6.8	9.6	12.9

2.　Create a new column named **Average** and enter a formula to work out the average temperature for **Brize Norton** over the six months. Copy this formula down the column to work out averages for the other locations.

3.　Format all numerical data to two decimal places.

4.　Centre the main heading across the top of the spreadsheet data and format to bold and italic.

5.　Save as **Temperature** and print a copy.

6.　Now delete the details for **Brize Norton** and make sure no empty cells remain.

7.　Insert a new row for **Lyneham** between **Oxford** and **Cambridge** and enter the following data:

Jan	Feb	Mar	Apr	May	Jun
3.9	3.5	6.0	7.7	11.1	14.1

8.　Work out the average temperature in **Lyneham** during the six months.

9.　Head a new row **AVERAGE** and work out the average temperature in all the locations during January. Copy this formula along the row to work out averages for all the months and ensure they are formatted to two decimal places.

10.　Apply borders and shading and realign or format any headings as you like and then print a copy of the spreadsheet to fit one page.

11.　Update and close the file.

 Module 4 sections 4.3, 5.3 and 7.1

You need to know how to:

◗ Modify margins

◗ Use the **Edit | Replace** menu to search and amend cell entries

1. Create the following spreadsheet showing costs for boat hire and save as Boats.

BOAT HIRE					
No. of people	1 Day	2 Day	3 Day	Weekly	Average
2 – standard boat	80	120	180	240	
2 – superior boat	100	130	250	280	
4 – standard boat	125	155	210	295	
4 – superior boat	150	180	225	300	
6 – luxury	200	225	250	320	
8 – standard	210	300	330	360	

2. Use a formula to work out the average daily rate for the two-person standard boat hired for a week (i.e. *Weekly rate divided by 7*).

3. Replicate this formula to work out average daily rates for all other boats.

4. Save and print a copy of the worksheet.

5. Centre the heading across the width of the spreadsheet.

6. The four-person standard boat is no longer available, so delete this entry completely.

7. The weekly cost for a six-person luxury boat should be changed to £375.

8. Insert a new row between the 2 – superior and 4 – superior boats for a special offer. The row heading should be Autumn special – 2-superior. Rates are as follows: 1 Day – £90; 2 Day – £125; 3 Day – £200 and Weekly – £265.

9. Widen columns as necessary to display all data fully and work out the average daily rate for the new entry.

10. Format the **Average** column to currency and no decimal places, but all other prices should be formatted to two decimal places. Realign any headings as preferred.

11. Using the **Edit** menu, replace each mention of **boat** with **class**, except in the spreadsheet title.

12. Ensure in Print Preview that the data are centred vertically on the page. Increase the left margin to 2 cm and make sure the spreadsheet will print on a single page.

13. Print the spreadsheet and close the file.

 Module 4 sections 2.6 and 7.1

EXERCISES 5 AND 6

You will need to know how to:

▶ Create a database

▶ Sort records

Exercise 5 1. Set up a spreadsheet to display information about homes for sale using the following column headings: Type, Bedrooms, Garage, Garden, Price, Location

Enter the following data:

Flat 4 bedrooms garage no garden £100,000 York

Bungalow 3 bedrooms garage garden £175,000 Selby

Flat 3 bedrooms no garage garden £97,000 York

Semidetached 4 bedrooms garage paddock £217,950 Derby

Detached 5 bedrooms garage garden £345,750 Nottingham

Bungalow 2 bedrooms garage patio garden £75,799 Selby

Flat 1 bedroom no garage no garden £115,000 Sheffield

Semidetached 3 bedrooms garage garden £200,450 York

2. Format the numerical data appropriately and add a border round the column headings before printing a copy. Save as **Homes**.

3. Sort the records by price in ascending order (from lowest to highest) and print a copy of the reordered spreadsheet.

4. Now carry out a first- and second-order sort: alphabetically by location and then by number of bedrooms in descending order. Save this change and print a copy.

5. Add the following record:

Detached house in Selby, price £300,990, 5 bedrooms, double garage, marina.

6. Sort first alphabetically by type and then by ascending order of price.

7. Delete the entire record for Nottingham and print a final copy of the spreadsheet before saving and closing the file.

 Module 4 section 2.7

Exercise 6 1. You have bought a range of tins and packets and want to work out which is the healthiest food. Set up a database with the title Healthy Eating and the following five field names (category headings):

Item Weight (g) Kcals Fat Protein

2. Enter the data as follows:

Item	Weight (g)	Kcals	Fat	Protein
Baked beans	420	260	1.20	19.4
Sardines	90	156	8.1	20.7
Dried apricots	500	800	3	20.70
Peanut butter	340	2023	172.72	83.64
Tuna	132	120	0.28	28
Almonds	300	1842	150	63.3

3. Add a new column headed Kcals per 100 g and enter a formula to work out the figure for baked beans (i.e. *Kcals/weight × 100*).

4. Copy this formula down the column to work out Kcals per 100 g for all the items.

5. Now add two new columns headed Fat per 100 g and Protein per 100 g. Work out the amounts for baked beans (i.e. *Protein/weight × 100* and *Fat/weight × 100*) and then copy these formulae down the columns to calculate fat and protein content for 100 g of all the other food items.

6. Right align all column headings except Item and apply your own choice of AutoFormat.

7. Format the Weight and Kcal columns to Integer (no decimal places) and all other numerical data to two decimal places before printing a copy of the database.

8. Sort the records in ascending order of Kcals per 100 g to find the least fattening food.

9. Underneath the data, type and complete the following sentence formatted in bold: **The item of food with the least Kcals per 100 g is … .**

10. After saving the file, add the text Healthy Eating as a footer and insert the filename as a field into the header.

11. Save and print a copy of the worksheet displaying the data centred vertically and horizontally and fitting on a single page.

12. Sort the database to see which food items have the most protein per 100 g and least fat per 100 g before closing the file.

 Module 4 section 2.7

EXERCISES 7 AND 8

You will need to know how to:

◗ Create a simple chart

◗ Resize and move charts

◗ Print charts alone or with spreadsheet data

Exercise 7 1. Create the following spreadsheet and save as Results:

Name	Score
Smith	245
Green	199
White	278
Burton	362
Wooleroote	299
Sims	375
Haversham	204

2. Sort the records in alphabetical order.

3. Create a 2D column chart to display the scores and place it on the same sheet as the data. The title should be **Final Results in 1999**, the axes should be labelled **Names** and **Scores** and there should be no legend.

4. Resize the chart to display all the data fully and move it so that it does not obscure the spreadsheet data.

5. Print a copy of the chart together with the spreadsheet data and save and close the file.

6. Reopen **Shares** and create a simple line chart with the title **Share Prices January – May** to display share prices for the five-month period. The x-axis should be labelled **Months**, the y-axis labelled **Price** and the legend should show the different companies.

7. Place the chart on the same sheet, resize if necessary and print a copy of the chart only.

8. Update the file before closing.

 Module 4 section 6.1 and 7.3

Exercise 8 1. The following pens are available through mail order:

Ballpoint pens	Number in pack	Cost
Zebra	10	6.70
Berol pen set	12	24.51
Punchline	50	5.75
Zebra Jimnie Classic	2	1.78
Pilot rubber grip	12	12.25
Pentel superb	12	9.72
Papermate stick	50	8.09
Uni	12	7.20
Staedtler stick	10	1.70
Bic crystal	20	3.57

2. Create a spreadsheet and enter these details. Make sure the columns are wide enough to display the full entries.

3. Format the **Cost** column to currency and print a copy.

4. Insert a new column between **Ballpoint pens** and **Number in pack** headed **Cost of 1 pen**. Enter a formula to work out the cost of one **Zebra** ballpoint (i.e. *Cost/Number in pack*) and copy it down the column to find the cost of each type of pen.

5. Delete the entry for the **Berol pen set**, making sure you don't leave an empty row.

6. Add a footer showing your name and the date.

7. Use an AutoFormat or add borders and shading from the **Format** menu to improve the appearance of the spreadsheet, and print a copy.

8. Now create a pie chart on the same sheet showing the cost of one pen of each type. Resize if necessary, add a suitable title, include data labels and print a copy of the chart on its own.

9. Update and close the file.

 Module 4 sections 6.1 and 7.3

EXERCISES 9, 10, 11 AND 12

You will need to know how to:

◗ Format chart elements

◗ Change chart type

◗ Select non-adjacent cell ranges

Exercise 9 1. Create the following spreadsheet and save as Rugby:

Roverton Rugby Club			
First Quarter Income			
Description	January	February	March
Joining fees	4000	2000	1950
Club House	3700	5500	5500
Donations	350	0	275
Other	275	136	400
Monthly totals			

2. Enter a formula to work out the total income for January.

3. Copy this across the row to work out totals for the other months.

4. Add a new column headed Total and enter a formula to work out the total joining fees received during the quarter. Copy this formula down the column to work out totals for the other sources.

5. Create a bar chart showing the sources of income for January. Give the chart the title January Income, and label the vertical axis Source of income and horizontal axis Income (£).

6. Format the axis labels to italic. Realign the y-axis labels, e.g. from horizontal to a slant.

7. Select an alternative chart title font and move the title to a new position within the chart area.

8. Add your name as a footer and print a copy.

9. Change the chart to a pie chart, add a legend and label the sectors with the % income. Print a copy of the amended chart.

10. Now create a chart of any type on the same sheet to show only the source of income and the quarterly total. Format attractively and save and print just the chart.

11. Finally, on a separate sheet, create a comparative column chart showing the income for all three months. Format attractively and print a copy before saving and closing the file.

 Module 4 sections 2.2 and 6.1

Exercise 10 1. Create a spreadsheet based on the following data showing the audience share of different terrestrial television channels.

CHANNEL	%AUDIENCE
BBC 1	28
BBC 2	18
ITV	30
Channel 4	14
Channel 5	10

2. Use the data to produce a column chart with the title Television Share of Viewers, the x-axis labelled TV Channels and the y-axis labelled %Audience.

3. Print a copy of the chart only and save the file as TV.

4. Reformat the title to bold, underlined and the axes labels to italic.

5. Move the legend to the top, left-hand corner of the chart.

6. Save these changes and print a copy of the amended chart.

7. Now change the chart type to a pie chart. Format the data series to show both percentages and labels and delete the legend.

8. Make other changes to colours and labels as required to make the chart clearer.

9. Print a copy of the pie chart and update and close the file.

 Module 4 sections 2.2 and 6.1

Exercise 11 1. Open the file Temperature and create a line graph on the same sheet as the spreadsheet to display the overall average temperature for each of the months.

2. Make sure that the x-axis displays the names of the months, and the y-axis shows the temperatures. Label the x-axis Months and the y-axis Temperature °C.

3. Format the y-axis labels to show zero decimal places, and remove the legend.

4. Resize the chart and any fonts to display the data clearly.

5. Give the chart the title Average Temperatures.

6. Change the colour of the plot area and select an alternative marker style on the line.

7. Save and print a copy of the chart together with the spreadsheet data.

8. Now create a comparative chart of any type to show the January to June temperatures for all the locations. Format any elements to improve the appearance of the chart and print a copy without the spreadsheet data visible.

9. Update and close the file.

 Module 4 sections 2.2 and 6.1

Exercise 12 1. Create the following spreadsheet showing examination passes and save it as Exams:

Name	English	French	Mathematics	Total	Overall %
Jameson	34	18	26		
Renshaw	26	15	31		
Fuller	25	16	23		
George	31	19	28		
Hardacre	29	21	23		
Smithson	35	20	33		

2. Enter a formula to work out the Total score achieved by Jameson and copy this down the column to work out totals for all students.

3. The maximum marks available in each subject are as follows: English – 38; French – 25; and Mathematics – 35. In cell *A11* enter a formula to add these figures and work out the maximum score possible.

4. Now find Jameson's overall **percentage**, using the formula: *Total/Maximum score* × *100*. Make sure you refer to cell *A11* in the formula and *not* the actual figure. Copy this formula down the column to work out everyone's overall percentage. Format the results to one decimal place.

5. Create a pie chart on the same worksheet entitled **Class Marks 2002** showing just the students' names and their overall percentage results. Ensure that the data is clearly labelled and displayed and print a copy.

6. Change to a bar chart. On the **Scale** tab in the *Format* dialog box; change the minimum for the *y* axis to 50. Realign, resize, remove unnecessary labels and format as necessary to display the data effectively.

7. Print a copy of the chart before saving and closing.

 Module 4 sections 2.2 and 6.1

You will need to know how to:

▶ Copy spreadsheets or charts between worksheets

▶ Copy spreadsheets or charts into a separate application

▶ Rename worksheets

Exercise 13
1. Open **Exams** and change the name of the sheet holding the spreadsheet data to **Exam Results**. Copy the chart onto a new worksheet and rename the sheet **Exam Chart**.

2. Minimize Excel and open Word. Write the following letter:

Chalfont Senior School
West Widnes
Harnaton
HA15 3XP

(today's date)

Dear Parent

You will be pleased to learn that our 6th Form boys have done very well this term. They all sat their English, French and Mathematics examinations and have gained higher marks than the same set last year.

You may like to see the full details of their results and so these are set out below:

3. Now return to Excel and copy across the spreadsheet data.

4. Add the following sentence to your letter:

As you can see from the chart, Nigel Smithson fully justifies the prize for academic success and we look forward to seeing you at the award ceremony on the last day of term.

5. Return to Excel, click the **Exam Chart** sheet and copy the chart across. Finally, sign the letter:

Yours faithfully

Charles Belham

Headmaster

6. Save the file as **Chalfont** and print a copy before closing both Excel and Word.

 Module 4 sections 2.5, 3.1 and 6.1

Exercise 14

1. In Word, type the following text:

   NEW AMERICAN-STYLE SPORTS SCHOOL IN BOGNOR REGIS

   OUR MISSION

   To provide high quality customized education within a caring and flexible environment in support of sport. Customized education is the process by which learning takes place.

   We believe that learning should be:
   personalized where curriculum more closely reflects the real world;
   relevant with connections to real life;
   cross-curricular to more closely reflect the real world;
   flexible to accommodate the unique learning needs of students; and
   multi-dimensional to involve more than skills and content

   These students did particularly well last year:

2. Save the file as **Sports**.

3. Now minimize Word, open Excel and create the following spreadsheet:

Student	Cricket	Football	Tennis	Swimming	Total Score
James	45	27	55	14	
Peter	37	49	68	24	
Derek	49	34	49	28	
Samantha	33	28	78	18	
Noel	42	39	33	29	
Anne	29	14	67	35	

4. Enter a formula to total James' score and copy this formula down the column. Now add an extra column headed **Average** and work out the average score for all the students.

5. Create a stacked comparative chart showing the student names and sports data for tennis and football only. Alter the scale so the maximum is 120 and add appropriate chart and axes labels. Retain a legend.

6. Save and print a copy of the chart alone.

7. Now select the **Student** and **Average** columns only and use these details to create a new chart. Delete the legend, give the chart the title **Student Scores 2002**, and format it as attractively as possible.

8. Copy the chart onto a new worksheet and name this **Sports Chart**. Save this change.

9. Now paste the chart into your **Sports** document.

10. Update the document and print a copy before closing both applications.

EXERCISE 15

You will need to know how to:

▶ Use the IF, MAX and MIN functions

▶ Wrap text

▶ Apply font colour

1. Create the following spreadsheet and save as **Food Preferences**:

ITEM	TEST 1 %	TEST 2 %	TEST 3 %
Cheese	56	45	71
Pork sausage	67	93	87
Chocolate	78	61	67
Dried fruit	34	54	23
Steak	82	87	73
Tomato	54	65	38
Red wine	78	76	65

2. Add a column headed **Average Overall Score** and enter average results for all items. Format these to show no decimal places.

3. Add a final column headed **Final Result** and use an IF statement to enter the appropriate text. Those items gaining an average % of over 60 should show the word **liked**, and those under 60 should show the word **disliked**.

4. Wrap any heading text to show full entries, but keep columns narrow.

5. Format all headings to bold, font size 14 and right-align the entries in the **Final Result** column and all headings except **Item**.

6. Reformat the main text to font size 12. Colour entries in the final column red.

7. Save and print a final copy of the spreadsheet.

8. To practice using other functions, change the entries in the **Average Overall Score** column to display the maximum and then minimum test scores for each item of food.

 Module 4 sections 4.3 and 5.2

Databases

In this module you can practise setting up databases, creating tables with appropriate datatypes and adding and amending records. You will be tested on your ability to sort your database and search for records meeting a range of criteria. The module also tests your knowledge of creating forms and reports and customizing them in different ways.

Subjects covered in this section:

Advanced exercises   **ECDL module**

9–10	Using grouping and summary options in a report	**5.5.1**
11–13	Customizing forms and reports	**5.3.1 and 5.5.1**
14	Creating a relationship between tables; designing a two-table query	**5.2.4 and 5.4.2**

You will need to know how to:

▸ Create a database file

▸ Design a table with appropriate field names and datatypes

▸ Save a table

Exercise 1　1.　Open Access and create a database file named **Food**.

2.　Design a new table with the following field names and datatypes:

Field Name	Data Type
Main food	Text
Title	Text
Cooking (mins)	Number
Portions	Number
Calories	Number

3.　Save the table as **Recipes** but don't set a primary key.

4.　Close the table.

5.　Close the file but not Access.

6.　Create a new database file named **Furniture**.

Field Name	Data Types
Name	Text
Price	Currency
Discount offered	Yes/No
Colours available	Number
Code	Text

7.　Design a new table with the following field names and datatypes:

8.　Save the table as **Chairs** but don't set a primary key.

9.　Close the table.

10.　Close the file.

⟨ECDL⟩ **Module 5, sections 1.1 and 2.1**

Exercise 2 1. Create a new database file named Sailings.

2. Design a table with the following field names and datatypes:

Field Name	Data Type
Dates	Text
UK port	Text
French port	Text
Short stay (£)	Currency
Long stay (£)	Currency
Weekend extra (£)	Currency

3. Save as **sailing costs** but don't set a primary key.

4. Close the table and then reopen it in Design view.

5. Add two further field names: **Bicycle supplement** and **Fast supplement** and set both datatypes as Currency.

6. Now save and close the table and close the file.

 Module 5, sections 1.1 and 2.1

EXERCISES 3, 4 AND 5

You will need to know how to:

▶ Open a database saved previously

▶ Open a table and enter records

▶ Amend entries

▶ Delete records

▶ Widen columns

▶ Print a table in landscape orientation

Exercise 3 1. Open the Food database.

2. Open the Recipes table and enter the following records:

Main food	Title	Cooking (mins)	Portions	Calories
Cod	Cod with herbs	40	4	193
Lentils	Lentil chilli	30	6	170
Tuna	Tuna bean salad	12	4	185
Aubergine	Roast vegetable soup	90	8	150
Pasta	Pasta with pesto sauce	30	4	538
Banana	Banana ice-cream	10	4	176
Eggs	Chocolate soufflé	30	8	204

3. Make sure all details are fully displayed.

4. Print a copy of the table in landscape orientation.

5. Now make the following amendments: Cod with herbs takes 50 minutes to cook; a portion of Banana ice-cream provides 250 calories; and the main food in the soup is Red pepper.

6. Delete the entire record for Lentil chilli and print a copy of the amended table.

7. Close the table and then close Food.

 Module 5, sections 1.2, 2.1, 2.3, 6.1 and 6.2

Exercise 4 1. Open the Furniture database and then open the Chairs table.

2. Enter the following records:

Name	Price	Discount	Colours	Code
Adjustable typist	19.99	Yes	4	TEK
Gas-lift typist	26.99	Yes	4	TCGL
Delux gas-lift typist	39.99	Yes	5	1116
Bentwood operator	69.99	No	1	WDOPR
Contemporary operator	69.99	No	2	AGNELLO
Modern operator	59.99	Yes	4	BETA
Ergonomic	149.99	Yes	5	VKHBA
Multifunctional	119.99	Yes	5	1228
Continuous use	179.99	No	3	HCT

1. Widen columns to display all the data fully and then print a copy of the table in landscape orientation.

2. Now make the following changes: the Delux gas-lift typist chair costs £43.99; the Ergonomic chair comes in seven colours and there is no discount on the Multifunctional chair.

3. Delete the entire record for the Gas-lift typist chair.

4. Print a copy of the amended records and then close the table.

5. Close Furniture.

 Module 5, sections 1.2, 2.1, 2.3, 6.1 and 6.2

Exercise 5 1. Create a new database called For Sale and then design a table to hold the following records. Decide appropriate datatypes (keeping Year as Number) but do not set a primary key, and save the table as Bikes:

Make	Price (£)	Type	CC	Year	Details
AJS	5999	Big port	350	1927	Black finish
Ariel	1750	Leader	250	1973	Clock
BSA	5250	DB34	500	1954	TLS front brake
BSA	8500	Rocket Goldie	650	1963	Single owner 30 yrs
AJS	2350	185	500	1957	Chrome tank panels
Ariel	3750	VH Red Hunter	500	1954	Excellent condition
Ariel	1950	Leader	250	1961	Blue finish

2. Print a copy of the table.

3. Now make the following amendments: the Ariel Leader priced at £1750 was produced in 1963; The Ariel Leader priced at £1950 has a red finish; and the BSA DB34 is for sale at £5999.

4. Delete the complete record for the Rocket Goldie bike.

5. Print a copy of the amended records and then close the table.

6. Close the For Sale file.

 Module 5, sections 1.2, 2.1, 2.3, 6.1 and 6.2

You will need to know how to:

▶ Sort records

▶ Use **Edit | Find** and **Edit | Replace**

▶ Amend field names

Exercise 6

1. Open the Food database and then the Recipes table.

2. In design view, change the field name Portions to Portion number.

3. Sort the records in alphabetical order of Main food and print a copy of the reordered table.

4. Now sort the records in descending order of Calories.

5. Find the first record where the cooking time is 30 minutes and change this to 35 minutes. Find the next record for a 30 minute recipe and change the cooking time to 40 minutes.

6. Print a copy of the amended records.

7. Close the Food database.

8. Open the Furniture database and display details of all the chairs.

9. Sort the records in descending order of price.

10. Print a copy of the reordered records.

11. Using **Edit | Replace**, amend all records showing chairs available in five colours to now offer six colours.

12. Sort the records in alphabetical order of chair Names and print a copy of the amended table.

13. Close the Furniture database.

 Module 5, sections 2.3, 4.1 and 4.3

Exercise 7 1. Open Sailings and the Sailing costs table in design view and change the Fieldname **Dates** to **Month**.

2. Now enter the following records:

Month	UK Port	French port	Short stay	Long stay	Weekend	Bikes	Fast
Spt	Portsmouth	Caen	£62.00	£87.00	£8.00	£0.00	£7.50
March	Portsmouth	Caen	£110.00	£146.00	£13.50	£5.00	£0.00
Spt	Plymouth	Roscoff	£65.00	£90.00	£8.00	£0.00	£7.50
July	Portsmouth	St. Malo	£145.00	£189.00	£16.00	£5.00	£7.50
Aug	Portsmouth	St. Malo	£126.00	£166.00	£13.50	£5.00	£7.50
Aug	Plymouth	Roscoff	£115.00	£152.00	£13.50	£5.00	£7.50

3. Widen the columns to display the data fully and print a copy in landscape orientation.

4. Delete the entire record for Portsmouth – St. Malo in August.

5. Add two new records:

Month	UK Port	French port	Short stay	Long stay	Weekend	Bikes	Fast
July	Plymouth	Roscoff	£133.00	£173.00	£16.00	£5.00	£7.50
March	Portsmouth	St. Malo	£126.00	£166.00	£13.50	£5.00	£0.00

6. Bike supplements in July are now £9. Using **Edit | Find**, find the first July record and then tab across to change the appropriate **Bicycle** entry. Find the next July record and repeat the amendment.

7. Using the **Edit | Replace** menu, increase the short stay cost of sailing from Plymouth to Roscoff in August from £115 to £121.

8. Sort the records in alphabetical order of French ports and print a copy of the table.

9. Now sort the records in descending order of the long stay cost and print a copy of the reordered records.

10. Close the file.

 Module 5, sections 2.3, 4.1 and 4.3

You will need to know how to:

▶ Change field properties

▶ Add a primary key

Exercise 8
1. Create a new database file named College.

2. Design a table with the following field names and datatypes:

Field Name	Data Type
Subject	Text
Room	Text
Tutor ID	Text
Start time	Number
End time	Number
Day	Text
Class code	Text
Price	Currency

1. Set a primary key on the Class code field.

2. Change the field properties for Start time and End times to show numbers to two decimal places.

3. Change the Price field properties to show currency with 0 decimal places.

4. Save the table as Classes and enter the following records:

Subject	Room	Tutor ID	Start time	End time	Day	Class code	Price
English	B7	H31	2	4	Tues	E142	£32
French	C9	W38	7	9	Wed	F43	£25
Watercolour	H5	J12	7	9	Tues	P712	£45
Sculpture	H5	M20	6.30	8.30	Th	P714	£85
IT	B7	M43	9.30	11.30	Mon	C24	£35
Spanish	C9	W38	7	9	Mon	S21	£25
Yoga	A15	M20	2.30	4.30	Th	Y2	£32
Business	B7	M43	2	4.30	Fr	B19	£25

5. Sort the records in alphabetical order of subject.

6. Amend the records so that **Watercolour** classes start at **6.30**, and **Spanish** is on **Fridays** and not **Mondays** and then print a copy in landscape orientation.

7. Close the table but not the file.

8. Now design a new table showing details of tutors with the following field names and data types:

Field Name	Data Type
First name	Text
Surname	Text
Subject 1	Text
Subject 2	Text
Telephone	Text
Tutor ID	Text

9. Set the primary key on **Tutor ID**.

10. Change the field size for the **Telephone** field to 7.

11. Save the table as **Tutors** and enter the following records:

First name	Surname	Subject 1	Subject 2	Telephone	Tutor ID
Mary	Harris	English	Business	0154752	H31
Diana	West	French	Spanish	0154851	W38
Peter	Jenkins	Painting	Collage	0154781	J12
Harry	Monks	Sculpture	Yoga	0154858	M20
Janet	Morrison	Computing	Business	0154732	M43

11. Sort the records in alphabetical order of surname and print a copy of the table.

12. Using **Edit | Replace**, make the following changes: Ms Morrison's first name is Jean; Peter Jenkins' ID should be J23; and Diana West's telephone number has changed to 0154233.

13. Close the table and then close the **College** database file.

 Module 5, sections 2.2 and 2.3

Exercise 9 1. Create a database named **Music** and design a table with the following structure:

Field Name	Data Type	Properties
Composer	Text	
Initials	Text	Field size 8
Title	Text	
Key	Text	Field size 15
Year born	Number	
Nationality	Text	
Price of CD (£)	Number	2 decimal places
Code	Text	

2. Set a primary key on **Code** and save the table as **Composers**.

3. Enter the following records:

Composer	Initials	Title	Key	Year born	Nationality	Price of CD (£)	Code
Beethoven	L. Van	Choral Symphony	D minor	1770	German	2.50	B5
Grieg	E	Peer Gynt Suite	N/A	1834	Norwegian	3.75	G3
Vivaldi	A	Spring	E major	1675	Italian	2.49	V2
Chopin	F	Piano Concerto no. 3	E minor	1810	Polish	3.99	C7
Bach	J.S	Brandenburg Concerto no. 1	F major	1685	German	7.50	B9
Schubert	F	Unfinished Symphony	B minor	1797	Austrian	2.95	S3

4. Print a copy of the records in landscape orientation.

5. Now make the following amendments using the **Edit | Replace** menu:
   - The Bach CD costs £8.99.
   - The Chopin Concerto should be no. 1.

6. Delete the entire record for **Grieg** and add a new record:

Mozart	W.A	Salzburg Symphony no. 2	B flat major	1756	Austrian	5.35	M6

5

7. Sort the records in alphabetical order of composer and print a copy of the table.

8. Using the **Edit** menu, find the first record for a **German** composer, and then find the second record.

9. Sort the records in descending order of year in which they were born and print a copy of the table before closing the file.

 Module 5, sections 2.2 and 2.3

EXERCISES 10, 11, 12 AND 13

You will need to know how to:

◗ Filter by selection to find records meeting one criterion

◗ Filter by form to find records meeting more than one criteria

◗ Use a range of expressions when filtering

Exercise 10 1. Create a database named **Children** and design a suitable table to display the following records. Save the table as **CD-ROMs**:

Title	Price (£)	Minimum age	Website	Rating
Games 3	10	7	www.tivola.co.uk	4
Identikit	10	7	www.planetdist.co.uk	2
Scrabble	13	12	www.johnlewis.com	3
Photo Expert	25	10	www.sierrahome.co.uk	3
Pop-up Dictionary	30	7	www.oup.co.uk	4
Card Studio	23	12	www.hallmark.co.uk	3
Heist	30	15	http://heist.vie.co.uk	2
Physicus	18	8	www.tivola.co.uk	4

2. Sort in ascending order of **Minimum age** and then print a copy of the table in landscape orientation.

3. Use a filter to find only those records with a rating of 4. Print a copy of the records and then remove the filter.

4. Sort the records in ascending order of price.

5. Now use a filter to find only those CD-ROMs that cost under £20 and are suitable for children under 9.

6. Print the records and then remove the filter and close the file.

 Module 5, section 4.1

Exercise 11 1. Open the College database and use a filter to find all the classes held on Tuesday.

2. Print a copy of the records and then remove the filter.

3. Sort the records in ascending order of Start times.

4. Now use a filter to find any classes being held in room B7 that start at 2 p.m.

5. Print a copy of the records displayed and then close the Classes table.

6. Open the Tutors table and use a filter to find any tutors who can teach Yoga. Print a copy of the records and then remove the filter.

7. Now sort the table in alphabetical order of Subject 1.

8. Use a filter to find the tutor whose ID begins with M and whose second subject is Business.

9. Print a copy of the record and then close the College file.

 Module 5, section 4.1

Exercise 12 1. Open the Sailings file and then the sailing costs table.

2. Use a filter to display all sailings to Roscoff and print a copy of the records.

3. Now find all sailings from Portsmouth that cost £90–£130 for a short stay. Print a copy of the records.

4. Finally, search for any sailings to St. Malo in March and print a copy before closing the file.

 Module 5, section 4.1

Exercise 13 1. Open **Music** and use a filter to search for any pieces of music in the key of E. Print a copy of the records.

2. Find any recordings that cost less than £5 and were written by a **German** or **Austrian** composer, and print the records.

3. Finally, print out details of any composers born after **1700** whose names begin with B.

4. Close the table and the file.

 Module 5, section 4.1

EXERCISES 14, 15 AND 16

You will need to know how to:

▶ Use a query to search for records

▶ Use a range of expressions when querying

▶ Save a query

▶ Hide fields in a query

Exercise 14 1. Create a database named **Outings** and then design a table to hold the following details of various activities taking place in the summer. Make sure the dates are **Date** datatypes (they can be displayed with the year or customized to show only days and months). Save the table as **Activities**.

Activity	Place	Start date	Duration (days)	Adult price (£)	Child price (£)	Family ticket
Flower show	Hampton Park Palace	9 July	3	17	5	Yes
Open day	Ramsgate Harbour	30 July	1	0	0	No
Creatures of the Night	Leighton Moss Nature Reserve	25 June	1	3	1	No
Arthurian antics	Pickering Castle	4 August	2	3.60	1.80	Yes
King for a day	Legoland	25 July	2	16	13	Yes
Puppet picnic	Grey's Court, Henley	30 July	1	5	0	No
Tortoises and turtles	Rescue Centre, Highbridge	18 June	2	4.75	3.50	No

2. Sort the records in alphabetical order of Activity and print a copy in landscape orientation, first making sure all data is fully displayed.

3. Now use a query to find all the activities taking place after 15 July. Display the Activity, Place and Start date only.

4. Print a copy of the records and save the query as Late summer.

5. Now search for all activities where a Family ticket is available. Show all the fields except Family ticket and Duration.

6. Print the results of the search and save the query as Family tickets.

7. Make the following changes to the table: the Puppet picnic is cancelled so the record needs to be removed completely; and add the Teddy Bears' Parade taking place in Richmond Park on 1 August. It costs £2.50 for adults, £1.50 for children, lasts a single day and a family ticket is available.

8. Close the table.

9. Now open the Family tickets query and check that it includes the Teddy Bears' Parade.

10. Print the query and then close the Outings file.

 Module 5, section 4.2

Exercise 15
1. Open the Furniture database.

2. Use a filter to find all chairs that cost more than £120 and print a copy of the records.

3. Sort the table alphabetically by Name and save this change.

4. Close the table and design a query to find all chairs offering a discount that come in more than 2 colours. Display only the Name and Price fields and save the query as Colourful.

5. Return to the design of the query and add the Code field. Then sort the records in descending order of Price before printing a copy.

6. Now use the * symbol to search for all chairs with a code beginning with the number 1 and display just the Name, Colours available and Price fields.

7. Save as Numerical Codes and print a copy.

5

8. Open the table and enter the following four new records:

    Comfort, £189.99, no discount, 4 colours, code COMFORT; Ultimate Executive, £229.99, no discount, 4 colours, code BBAS; Chrome Managers, £79.99, discount available, 5 colours, code CHRM; and Wood Executive, price £169.99, 1 colour, no discount and code 1314A5.

9. Design a new query to find all chairs costing more than £120 that are available in 4 or more colours. Display the name, price and code fields only and save the query as Chairs over £120.

10. Finally reopen the Numerical Codes query and check that the Wood Executive chair is now listed. Print a copy and then close the file.

 Module 5, section 4.2

Exercise 16
1. Open the Food database and search for all recipes that take less than 15 minutes to cook. Print a copy of the records showing only the Main food, Title and Cooking time. Save the query as Quick recipes.

2. Now add the following recipes to the table:
    - Rhubarb is the main food in a Crumble recipe that takes 40 minutes to cook, provides 8 portions and 192 calories per portion.
    - Flour is the main ingredient for Pizza that takes 20 minutes to cook, provides 4 portions and 375 calories in each portion.

3. Sort the table in ascending order of Calories per portion.

4. Search for all recipes for four or more people at less than 200 calories per portion. Sort alphabetically by Title, display just the Title, Cooking time and Calories and save as Under 200 calories.

5. Print a copy of the query and then close the file.

 Module 5, section 4.2

ADVANCED EXERCISES

EXERCISE 1

You will need to know how to:

- Create a validation rule
- Set up an index

1. Create a new file named Tennis and design the following table:

Field Name	Data Type	Properties
Membership No	AutoNumber	
Category	Text	
Surname	Text	
Firstname	Text	
Joining date	Date	Medium date
Female	Yes/No	

2. Set up an index on the Surname field, and allow duplicates.

3. The Category field should only accept the text Senior, Junior or Concession. Set this for the Validation Rules field and enter appropriate validation text to appear if the rule is not met.

4. Save the table as Members and enter the following records. Try to enter the Category of Diane Brown as 'Temporary' before typing the correct entry.

Membership No	Category	Surname	Firstname	Joining Date	Female
1	Senior	Brown	Joan	22-May-01	Yes
2	Junior	Brown	Terry	22-May-01	No
3	Junior	Brown	Madge	22-May-01	Yes
4	Senior	Bergot	Francis	18-June-01	Yes
5	Senior	Wilson	Harold	22-June-01	No
6	Senior	Brown	Peter	28-June-01	No
7	Junior	Brown	Diane	28-June-01	Yes
8	Concession	Hill	Susan	01-July-01	Yes
9	Senior	Harper	Graeham	04-July-01	No
10	Junior	Harper	Sally	04-July-01	Yes

5. Search the database for Madge Brown and display her full name, Category and Joining Date only. Print out the details.

6. Now search the database for anyone named Brown who joined before 1st June, sort alphabetically by first name and display only their Firstname, Joining Date and Membership No. Save the query as Brown in May.

7. Print a copy of the query displaying its name on the printout.

8. Finally, search for any male members in the **Senior** category and display only **Firstname, Surname** and **Joining Date**. Sort alphabetically by **Surname** and save as **Senior Males**.

9. Print a copy of the records and then close the file.

 Module 5, sections 2.2 and 2.3

EXERCISE 2

You will need to know how to:

▶ Amend the design of a query

1. Open the **College** file and then search the **Tutor** table to find which tutors teach **Business**. Display their Firstnames and Surnames only.

2. Save the query as **Business Tutors** and print a copy.

3. Using the same query, amend it so that you search for tutors who teach **Business** or **Computing**. Display *all* their **Subjects**, their **Surnames**, and add their **Telephone Numbers**.

4. Print a copy of the amended query and save the changes.

5. Now search for any classes that cost between £20 and £30 and print details of the **Subject, Room** and **Day** only. Save as **Classes from £20 – £30**.

6. Amend the query to display the same price range of classes but remove the **Room** field and add **Start** and **End** times. Save the changes and print a copy before closing the file.

 Module 5, section 4.2

You will need to know how to:

▶ Create a form using the AutoForm function

▶ Design a form using the Wizard

▶ Use a form for entering and amending records

▶ Print selected records

Exercise 3 1. Open the Children database and design a new table named Books to hold the following records:

Title	Author	Publisher	Price	Recommended age
Terrific I'm a Tarantula	Bradman	Bloomsbury	6.75	7
Public Enemy No. 2	Horowitz	Walker	3.99	12
I don't like Space Glop	Matthews	Bloomsbury	4.50	5
The Five Sisters	Mahy	Scholastic	4.99	8
Storm	Fisher	Collins	9.99	11
When the Forest meets the Sea	Baker	Walker	4.99	4

2. Sort the records alphabetically by Author and print a copy of the table.

3. Now create a Columnar AutoForm based on this table.

4. Use the form to add the following records:

   ● Scary Stories by Helen Paiba, aimed at 9 year olds and published by Macmillan at £6.99
   ● Star Wars Episode 1 by George Lucas, published by Scholastic at £4.99 aimed at children at least 7 years old.

5. Use the form to display the record for Storm and print a copy of this record only.

6. Use the form to make the following amendments:

   ● Public Enemy No. 2 is suitable for 9 year olds
   ● The Five Sisters is published by Puffin
   ● Bradman's book costs £3.99.

7. Close the form and save it as Books AutoForm.

8. Open the table and print a copy of the amended records.

9. Now design a new form using the Wizard with only the following fields selected in order: Author, Title, Price and Publisher.

10. Save as Wizard Books Form, open the form and print one record.

11. Close the Children file.

Exercise 4

1. Open the Food file and design an AutoForm based on the Recipes table. Save it as Recipe form.

2. Use the form to add the following recipes:
   - Macaroni Cheese, main food pasta, takes 25 minutes to cook, enough for 6 people and provides 280 calories per portion.
   - Borscht, main food beetroot, feeds 10 people at 102 calories per portion, and takes 30 minutes to cook.

3. With the form open, delete the record for Banana Ice-cream.

4. Use the form to make the following changes:
   - Cod with herbs takes 60 minutes to cook;
   - there are 410 calories in each portion of chocolate soufflé;
   - change pesto sauce to tomato sauce.

5. Design a new form using the Wizard that has a different layout and background to the AutoForm you produced, and save it as Wizard recipe form.

6. Go to the recipe for Tuna salad and print a copy of the form displaying only this record.

7. Close the form and the database file.

Exercise 5

1. Open the Tennis database and create a form of your choice using the Form Wizard.

2. Use it to add the following new members:

   Shirley Webb, Concession, Female, Joined 3 August
   Martin Piller, Senior, Male, Joined 15 August.

3. Print a copy of the form showing one of the new records only.

4. Use the form to make the following amendments:
   - Graeham spells his name Graham
   - Joan Brown joined on 24 May
   - Francis Brown is male.

5. Close the form and check that the new records and amendments have been added to the table.

6. Design a query to find out joining dates of all senior members. Include only the dates, surnames and membership numbers.

7. Save as **Seniors** and print a copy before closing the file.

 Module 5, sections 3.1 and 6.2

EXERCISES 6, 7 AND 8

You will need to know how to:

▶ Create a report using the AutoReport function

▶ Design a report using the Wizard

Exercise 6 1. Open the **Furniture** database and create an AutoReport in table format based on the **Chairs over £120** query. Give it the same name as the query.

2. Save the report and print a copy.

3. Open the table and sort the records in ascending order of price.

4. Design a report in table format using the wizard which is based on the table and where only the following fields are displayed: **Name**, **Price** and **Code**. Name the report **Chairs 2002** and print a copy.

5. Use a query to find all chairs aimed at **executives** or **operators** that cost between £70 and £200. Decide which fields to display and save as **Op** or **Exec chairs**.

6. Create a report based on this query and print a copy.

7. Close the **Furniture** database.

 Module 5, section 5.1

Exercise 7 1. Open the database holding information about motorbikes.

2. Search for all bikes that are under £5000 built before 1962 and display all the fields except the **Year**.

3. Save the query as **Pre-1962 Bikes**.

4. Now create a report based on this query using the Wizard. Place the fields in the following order: Make, Price, Type, CC and then Details and give it the same name as the query.

5. Print a copy of the report.

6. Close the report and design a new table named Cars to hold the following records:

    £11800 97 R Saab 4 door, midnight blue, climate control from Oxford Saab
    £6695 98 S Rover 5 door, Oxford blue, alloys from Kernahan MG
    £15850 99 T Saab 4 door, black, CD player from Oxford Saab
    £7995 98 R Vauxhall Vectra 5 door, red, air conditioning from Autopark
    £8995 94 M Corrado 3 door, metallic red, full leather from Autopark
    £6990 97 R Honda Civic 5 door, silver, twin airbags from Kernahan MG
    £5995 98 R Peugeot 5 door, cherry red, tinted glass from Autopark
    £14995 99 V Mazda 5 door, black, only 2000 miles from Motorworld

7. Sort in ascending order of Price and print a copy of the records.

8. Search for all black or red cars that are post-1997 and display their Price, Make, Colour, Rgistration letter, Special features and Dealer name only. Save the query as Newer Cars and print a copy.

9. Finally, produce a report based on this query and print a copy before closing the For Sale database file.

 Module 5, section 5.1

Exercise 8 1. Open the Tennis database and create a query to display only the female members of the club.

2. Save as Female members.

3. Using the Wizard, create a report based on this query. The fields should be displayed in the following order, and you should not include Membership No or Female:

    Firstname   Surname   Joining Date   Category

4. Save and print a copy of the report.

5. Now create an AutoReport – Tabular report based on the complete table.

6. Save as Membership Details and print a copy before closing the file.

 Module 5, section 5.1

You will need to know how to:

▶ Design a report that uses grouping or summary options

Exercise 9
1. Open **Outings** and design a report showing the various activities grouped by date (you may want to see the effect of changing the grouping options so that they are by day and not month). Give it the name **Activities Over the Summer**.

2. Print a copy of the report and then close the file.

3. Now open **Children** and design a query based on the **CD-ROMs** table to show all fields except **Rating**.

4. Design a report based on this query that groups the records by **Minimum age** and then print a copy of the report before closing the file.

5. Finally, open any other database and create a report that groups the records in some way, e.g. books by publisher, bikes by make or classes by day.

6. Save and print a copy of the report before closing the file.

 Module 5, section 5.1

Exercise 10
1. Create a new **Jobs** database and design the following table saved as **Job Details**:

Field Names	Data Types
Employer	Text
Job	Text
Salary	Currency
Location	Text
Contact	Text
Closing date	Date

5

2. Enter the following details into the table:

Employer	Job	Salary	Location	Contact	Closing date
Connell	Sales	£18,000.00	Oxford	01865 76333	20/02/02
St. Mary's	RE teacher	£23,000.00	Milton Keynes	01844 22366	15/02/02
Hedges	Secretary	£16,500.00	Oxford	01865 56699	01/03/02
Mango	Administrator	£17,500.00	Oxford	01865 44455	20/02/02
Buildbase	Sales	£24,000.00	Witney	01993 23111	03/03/02
Garsington	Education Officer	£14,000.00	Abingdon	01235 22288	14/02/02

3. Design a query to display only Oxford jobs, and show all fields except Location, Closing date and Contact.

4. Save and print a copy of the query.

5. Return to the table and delete the Milton Keynes record entirely and increase the salary for Hedges to £17,950.

6. Add the following two records:

   Beaumont House, Care Assistant, £12,500, Abingdon, 01235 44777, 14/2/02
   Gateway Hotel, 2nd Chef, £19,000, Witney, 01993 22134, 5/3/02.

7. Design a report to show all fields except Contact and group data by Location. Use the summary option to include the average salaries for each location and save as Average.

8. Print a copy of the report and close the file.

 Module 5, section 5.1

EXERCISES 11, 12 AND 13

You will need to know how to:

▶ Customize forms and reports

Exercise 11 1. Open your Recipe AutoForm.

2. In design view, add a large form heading label, type in RECIPES and make the font bold, 14 point.

3. Change the fill colour of the controls.

4. Format the text labels to italic.

5. Resize any of the controls to display the entry more clearly.

6. Print a copy of one record in form view and then close the file.

 Module 5, sections 3.1 and 5.1

Exercise 12 1. Open the report Membership Details.

2. In design view, reposition any headings so that they sit more clearly over the data, and resize if necessary to display the complete entry.

3. Change the title to Tennis Club Members and reformat the font type and size.

4. Change the Membership No. label to Number.

5. Add your name to the page footer.

6. Print a copy of the report and close the file.

 Module 5, sections 3.1 and 5.1

Exercise 13 1. Open the Average report in the Jobs database in Design view.

2. Delete the extra wording beginning summary for location ... .

3. Amend the Avg label to read Average salaries and format to italic.

4. Ensure that all column headings are clearly visible.

5. Reformat any headings, e.g. change the report label font or give it initial capital letters.

6. Print a copy of the report before saving and closing the file.

 Module 5, sections 3.1 and 5.1

5

You will need to know how to:

▶ Create a relationship between tables

▶ Design a two-table query

1. Create a database with the name **Sunsoak Holidays**. Design a table saved as **Villas**, setting a primary key on Code. (The data type should be Text to display zeros.) Enter the records as shown:

Name	Code	Country	Price (£)	Maximum No.
Nachtag	0011	Germany	276	5
Der Haus	0015	Germany	223	6
La Musique	0022	France	114	2
Flowers	0023	France	150	6
La Girande	0027	France	286	6
Le Pont	0046	France	245	8
High House	0062	Ireland	125	3
The Mill	0065	Ireland	134	4

2. Now create a second table, **Bookings**, with a primary key on Booking Number. This should have an AutoNumber data type.

Booking Number	Date taken	Name	Contact	Code	Month required
1	02/02/03	Marlow	01235 67584	0011	October
2	22/02/03	Johnson	01491 39987	0046	September
3	13/03/03	Hepple	01865 22114	0065	August
4	02/04/03	Smith	01865 33445	0011	July
5	03/04/03	Binns	01865 54838	0062	August
6	04/04/03	Paterson	01865 47738	0046	May
7	12/05/03	Black	01235 19876	0023	July
8	21/05/03	Thomson	01235 67584	0027	June

3. Sort the Villas table in ascending order of Country and print a copy.

4. Search for all French villas, then save and print a copy of the query.

5. Print a copy of all bookings taken before May, showing only the date, name and contact number.

6. Now create a relationship between the two tables, linking the Villa code in each table.

7. Create a query based on fields from both tables to show details of all bookings in France for summer holidays, i.e. June, July or August. Display only the client's name, contact numbers, month required, villa name and price.

8. First save as **Summer French Villas** and then print a copy that will now show the query name.

9. Close the database.

 Module 5, sections 2.4 and 4.2

5

Presentation

This module includes exercises covering the main features of the presentation package PowerPoint. You need to be able to add text, images and objects to slides; customize backgrounds, and include transitions and animations when running a presentation on the computer. You can also test your knowledge of how to create organization or numerical charts and print a range of objects including notes pages and handouts.

Subjects covered in this section:

Introductory exercises		ECDL module
1–2	Creating a basic presentation	**6.1.1 and 6.6.2**
3	Moving and formatting text; changing to portrait orientation	**6.3.1, 6.3.3 and 6.6.1**
4	Changing line spacing	**6.3.1**
5–6	Adding, moving and resizing images	**6.3.2 and 6.3.3**
7	Adding and editing WordArt; formatting text boxes	**6.4.3**
8	Copying and pasting objects within slides	**6.4.4**
9–10	Adding slides; moving between slides; reordering slides; changing slide layout; bullets	**6.2.2, 6.3.1 and 6.6.1**
11	Duplicating slides; copying and pasting images between slides	**6.3.3 and 6.6.1**
12–13	Inserting and formatting AutoShapes; rotating, flipping and layering objects; printing selected slides	**6.4.3 and 6.6.2**
14	Applying different line weights and styles to text boxes	**6.4.3**

You need to know how to:

▶ Start a new presentation

▶ Work in different views

▶ Use placeholders or text boxes to insert text

▶ Save and print slides

▶ Close a presentation

Exercise 1

1. Open PowerPoint and start a new presentation.

2. Select a bulleted list or title slide layout.

3. In Slide view enter the following title: Transport.

4. Click in the list box and add the following text as a list: Cars, Buses, Walking, Bicycles.

5. Go to Outline view and insert the word Trains after Cars.

6. Change to Normal view and use a text box to add the following text above the title: My first talk.

7. Add a further text box above the list and type: Topics that will be covered.

8. Save the presentation as Transport and print a copy of the slide before closi

 Module

Exercise 2

1. Sta ... yout.

2. In ... xt: Beware of the Dog.

3. C ... Type the following:

   N ... Ve only read material we

   ł ... y to waste paper.

4. ... closing the presentation.

6

 Mo

EXERCISE 3

You will need to know how to:

- Move text boxes
- Format text
- Change to portrait orientation

1. Start a new presentation. Select a blank slide layout.
2. Add the following title: Car Boot Sale
3. Below this, add the text: Come to 14 Greenacres and find a bargain!
4. Centre both entries.
5. Move the title below the address.
6. Change the text to Brilliant Car Boot Sale formatted to font size 40 point, and format the address to italic, 32 point.
7. Change to portrait orientation and reposition and re-size the text boxes if necessary so that they are centrally placed in the top half of the slide.
8. Save as Car Boot and print a copy of the slide before closing the file.

 Module 6, section 3.1, 3.3 and 6.1

EXERCISE 4

You need to know how to:

- Change line spacing

1. Reopen Transport.
2. Select the main title and format it to bold and underlined with a shaded effect.
3. Select the list and format this to italic.
4. Increase the line spacing within the list.
5. Centre My first talk and increase the font so that it is slightly larger than the title text.

6. Make Topics that will be covered bold and font size 18 point.

7. Save these changes and print an amended copy of the slide before closing the presentation.

 Module 6, section 3.1

EXERCISES 5 AND 6

You will need to know how to:

◗ Add images to a slide

◗ Move and resize images

Exercise 5 1. Start a new presentation and select a slide with Clip Art and text place-holders.

2. Make the title of the slide Gardens and format it attractively.

3. Double-click the Clip Art placeholder and find and insert an image of a plant.

4. Add the following text as a list:

   Plan carefully, Provide seats, Add fragrant and colourful flowers, Include a water feature.

5. Save as Gardens and print a copy of the slide.

6. Now reduce the size of the image by half and move it to a different position on the slide.

7. Insert a second gardening image, resized so that it matches the size of the first image, and position it somewhere on the slide.

8. Make any further changes to text or images as you like and then save and print a copy of the updated slide.

9. Close the presentation.

 Module 6, sections 3.2 and 3.3

Exercise 6 1. Reopen Notice.

2. Format the main heading in bold and increase the font size.

3. Apply a dark colour to the text.

4. Select the main text and format to italics.

5. Insert an image of a dog or newspaper, and print a copy of the slide.

6. Resize the image and position it in the top, right-hand corner of the slide. If necessary, resize or move text boxes so that all text is clearly displayed.

7. Save this change and print a revised version of the slide before saving and closing.

 Module 6, sections 3.2 and 3.3

EXERCISE 7

You will need to know how to:

▶ Add WordArt to a slide*

▶ Make changes to a WordArt object

▶ Format text boxes

1. Start a new presentation, select a blank slide layout and change to portrait orientation.

2. You are going to produce a poster advertising a concert. Insert a musical Clip Art image and the text **Schubert's Symphony No. 8 in B minor** anywhere on the slide, and then save as **Concert**.

3. Add two further text boxes that will display details of the date/time – **Saturday, 23 May at 8.00 p.m.** – and venue – **The Hopkins Great Hall** – in differently formatted text.

4. Select and insert an appropriate WordArt title: **Concert Series**. Move it so that it appears at the top of the slide, and resize or format the colours and shape to your liking.

5. Move the Clip Art image so that it appears at the bottom of the slide and re-arrange the text boxes so that all the details are attractively arranged.

6. Add borders and background colours to some of the text boxes.

7. Now edit the WordArt so that it reads: **Opening Concert**.

8. Update the presentation and print a copy of the slide before closing the file.

* Please note that WordArt is not a requirement of (or included in) the ECDL syllabus and can be replaced with text boxes.

 Module 6, section 4.3

You will need to know how to:

▶ Copy and paste objects within a slide

1. Reopen **Car Boot**.

2. Insert and format the following WordArt object: **Come Along on Saturday**. Place it under the text.

3. Copy the WordArt and paste it several times so that four or five sets of words fill the bottom half of the slide.

4. Insert an image of a chair or other item that might be found at a car boot sale. Resize it to fit in the top, right-hand corner of the slide.

5. Add a thick, coloured border to the image.

6. Edit one WordArt object so that it now reads: **You won't be sorry** and reformat it to contrast with those saying **Come Along on Saturday**.

7. Remove the border if it is showing round the address, but add a thick, coloured border and contrasting coloured background to the **Car Boot Sale** title.

8. Update the file and print a copy of the slide before closing.

 Module 6, section 4.4

You will need to know how to:

▶ Add new slides

▶ Move between slides

▶ Reorder slides

▶ Change slide layout

▶ Work with bullets

6

Exercise 9 1. Open your Transport presentation.

2. Add a new slide with placeholders for one left-hand text column and one Clip Art image.

3. Enter the title BUSES.

4. Click in the text column and type the following:

Advantages of buses:

Reading or sleeping as you travel
Less pollution
Season tickets can make this economical

5. Remove the subheading bullet point but retain bullets for the listed items.

6. Insert an image of a bus by double-clicking the placeholder.

7. Save the changes and print a copy of the slide.

8. Now change the slide layout to two text columns.

9. Move the image above the title and add this text in the right-hand column, formatted to match the first column:

Disadvantages of buses:

Waiting at bus stops
Expensive for families
Restricted times to travel

10. Add a third slide of any layout that has the title Walking in either normal text or WordArt.

11. Add three enjoyable reasons for taking walks and then insert a suitable Clip Art image.

12. Go back to the first slide and then add a new slide, slide 2, which will have the title CARS. Select any slide layout and just add the title.

13. Now move to Walking and insert a new slide 5 of any layout with the title Trains.

14. Change the slide order so that Trains appears between Cars and Buses.

15. Finally, add a slide 6 entitled Cycling and insert a suitable image. Save and close the file.

 Module 6, sections 2.2, 6.1 and 6.3

Exercise 10
1. Start a new presentation and insert three slides: two blank and the third with placeholders for text and Clip Art. Save as **Nature**.

2. Go to the first blank slide and insert an animal image.

3. Insert a WordArt object: **Birds and other Animals** above the image and add the following text:

   Presentation by Jane Wyckham, Milton Park Nature Reserve

4. Add a text box containing the following words:

   Friday 8.30–10.00 p.m. at Clarendon College, Brackley

5. Reformat the main and subheading text and add borders or shading to the text boxes.

6. Move through the slides until you reach slide 3.

7. Insert a flower picture, colour it yellow and add the title **Telling Flowers apart** followed by the following list of names:

   Coltsfoot, Ragworts, Hawkbits, Common fleabane and Sowthistle

8. Add a new slide 4 in two-column layout. Then enter the title **Pollution Signs** and, in one column, type:

   The Lichen Test

   None – bad air
   Small amounts – slightly better
   Long and shrubby – clean country air

9. In the other column, type the following list:

   Lifeless Water

   Sewage
   Oil
   Rubbish

10. Reorder the slides so that the flower slide is slide 4.

11. Go back to the blank slide and change the layout to display a title place-holder. Add a bird picture and the title: **Birds around Britain**.

12. Add further text boxes containing the names of different birds, such as **peregrine falcon, swallow, swan,** and **golden eagle**. Arrange these in a random fashion on the slide.

13. Format each text box and entry completely differently by using different font types and sizes and adding coloured backgrounds and borders.

14. Print a copy of all four slides and then save and close the presentation.

 Module 6, sections 2.2 and 6.1

You will need to know how to:

▶ Duplicate slides

▶ Copy and paste images between slides

1. Start a new presentation and select a blank slide layout.

2. Insert the text *Decisions to Make* centrally on the slide, formatted to Arial, 44 point, bold.

3. Underneath, add the text: *What do you like to do?* Increase the font size and format in italic.

4. Now duplicate the slide twice to create two extra slides.

5. Go to slide 2 and change the question to *What are you good at?*

6. Go to slide 3 and change the question to *Will you fit in?*

7. Return to the first slide and add a Clip Art image of shaking hands (or other picture suitable for a presentation on getting a job). Resize if necessary and move it to the bottom, centre of the slide.

8. Copy this image onto the other slides.

9. Add a new slide to become slide 1, in title slide layout.

10. Enter the following text: *Tips on Job Interviews* and apply appropriate formatting.

11. Save as **Jobs** and print a copy of the presentation before closing the file.

 Module 6, sections 3.3 and 6.1

You will need to know how to:

▶ Insert and format AutoShapes

▶ Rotate, flip and layer objects

▶ Print selected slides

▶ Use guidelines

Exercise 12 1. You are going to start preparing a presentation on The History of Britain. Select a title slide, a slide with an organization chart placeholder and a blank slide.

2. Return to the title slide and type The History of Britain as the main title and your name and today's month and year as a subtitle.

3. Insert an enlarged image of a clock or historical character and place it centrally on the slide, but *behind* the text. You may need to change the text colour to white or yellow so that it shows up clearly.

4. Near the bottom of the slide, add a block arrow AutoShape pointing to the left, with text above it that says Come this way through time.

5. Save as History and print one copy of the slide.

6. Now rotate or flip the arrow to point to the right.

7. Insert WordArt with the text History Comes Alive and place this at the top of the slide. Border it with an oval AutoShape filled with a contrasting colour, making sure the words are displayed clearly.

8. Save and print a copy of the title slide only before closing the file.

 Module 6, sections 4.3 and 6.2

Exercise 13 1. You are going to design a get well card. Start a new presentation, select the blank slide layout and change to portrait orientation.

2. Add guidelines using the **View** menu, if they are not already visible.

3. In the top, left-hand quarter (to become the inside of the card) insert the following in a text box:

With Very Best Wishes from Everyone in the Office

4. Realign the text and format the text size so that it fills most of the message area. Add colours and borders as you like.

5. Rotate or flip the box so that the wording is upside down.

6. In the bottom, right-hand quarter (the front of the card) add a picture on the theme of illness or injury.

7. Now add an arched WordArt object above the picture that says Sorry and a horizontal object below it that says You are ill.

8. Border the front of the card by adding a rectangular AutoShape with a colour fill. Make sure the text and picture are still clearly visible.

9. Save as Sorry.

10. Add the words **Get well soon** in the bottom left quarter of the slide and rotate it so that it will appear at a 45° angle across the back of the card.

11. Save this change and print a copy of the card before closing the file.

 Module 6, sections 4.3 and 6.2

EXERCISE 14

You will need to know how to:

▶ Apply different line weights and styles to text boxes

1. Create a four-slide presentation and save as **Villa**. Select a title slide and three blank slide layouts.

2. On the title slide, enter the following heading: **Villa For Sale**

3. Add a thick, black border.

4. Add the following subtitle text: **Sea Views and Luxury Fittings**

5. Border this text box in green, selecting a double or triple line style.

6. Format the text in both boxes so that it fills most of the main slide area.

7. Move to slide 2 and add the title **Location**. Underneath, add the following bulleted list:

  ● **Close to the seafront in sunny Portsmouth**
  ● **Near the shops and local schools**
  ● **Good road and rail links to London or the South West**
  ● **Ferries to the Isle of Wight or France always available.**

8. Format the bullets in an alternative style and border and shade the text box containing the list in dark red, dashed lines and weight 6 point.

9. Print a copy of slide 2 only.

10. Go to Slide 3 and change the slide layout to text plus Clip Art.

11. Insert a seaside-related image and border with a thick, coloured border.

12. Add the following text:

  The Villa has a large sitting room with south-facing balcony, two bedrooms with en suite shower room and pine fitted kitchen

13. Add a title: Villa Details as WordArt and position this centrally at the top of the slide.

14. Reorder slides 2 and 3.

15. Change the layout of slide 4 to a title only slide and add the title: Contact Information

16. Add a separate text box containing the address:

    Wilmotts Estate Agent, 23 Harrington Road, Portsmouth, Tel: 01705 666777

17. Border the address with an oval border and fill with colour, making sure the text is still clearly visible.

18. Reformat any text or objects to ensure each slide is attractively laid out, and then print a copy of the complete presentation.

19. Save and close the file.

 Module 6, section 4.3

ADVANCED EXERCISES

EXERCISES 1 AND 2

You will need to know how to:

● Add slide backgrounds

● Create and print a notes page

● Goup drawings

Exercise 1

1. Open Gardens.

2. Add a second slide with just a title placeholder and enter the following words:

   View from your Window.

3. Underneath, draw a simple picture of a window with the sun and some flowers inside. Use the rectangle, oval, etc., AutoShapes – Stars and Banners, or Flowchart shapes can provide flower heads – and colour them as appropriate. The following shows an example:

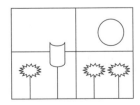

4. Select a green or brown background colour that either has an attractive pattern or other fill effect and apply it to both the slides in your presentation.

5. Reverse the order of your slides and amend the title text of slide 2 to Garden Planning.

6. Now create a Notes page for this slide and type the following notes:

College course starts 19 September
Address for enrolment forms
Book to read: 'Planning Your Garden' by Deirdre Wiseman

7. Print a copy of the Notes page and both slides.

8. Group your drawing, resize and move it to another part of the slide.

9. Save and close the presentation.

 Module 6, sections 2.2, 3.1 and 6.1

Exercise 2 1. Re-open Villa and apply a pale blue, graded colour background to all the slides.

2. Create a Notes page for the last slide and type the following:

Mention we are closed on Mondays.

Give out flyer on sister offices in Plymouth and Exeter.

Ask for names and addresses of anyone interested in viewing this or similar properties.

3. Print a copy of the Notes page only.

4. Duplicate the first slide and move the extra slide so that it become the last slide.

5. Change the background colour of this slide only to yellow, retaining the gradient.

6. Add a picture of a beach ball by using one crescent AutoShape, copying and flipping it horizontally and placing the two shapes together.

7. Colour two of the segments.

8. Group the shapes and move the ball to the top left of the slide.

9. Print a copy of the last slide only and then save and close the presentation.

 Module 6, sections 2.2, 3.1 and 6.1

EXERCISES 3 AND 4

You will need to know how to:

◗ Apply a design template

◗ Print handouts

Exercise 3
1. Open Nature.

2. Select a suitable design template with a brown or green main colour and apply to all the slides.

3. Go to the Birds around Britain slide and create a Notes page that includes reminders about an Owl Sighting evening; a conference on rare birds next Autumn in Inverness; and that cheap binoculars are available from Keswick Camera Stores.

4. Print just the Notes page.

5. Change the design template applied to the presentation.

6. Print a handout with all slides on one page.

7. Save and close the file.

 Module 6, sections 2.3 and 6.2

Exercise 4
1. Start a new presentation and select a slide layout with Clip Art and bulleted list placeholders.

2. Insert a picture relevant to holidays, e.g. suitcases, beach, aeroplane, etc.

3. Give the slide the title Holidays in India and save the file as Holiday.

4. Add the following list:

Vaccinations; Tickets; Packing for hot countries; Things to see

5. Add four new slides and insert one WordArt object on each slide as a title, with the wording taken from the list.

6

6. On the Vaccinations slide, find or draw a picture of a hypodermic needle similar to the one below and partly fill with colour. (Use Basic or Flowchart shapes as well as lines.)

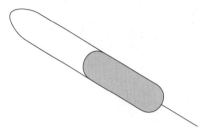

7. Group the drawing and rotate it so that it is at an angle.

8. On the *Things to See* slide, add the following text in separate text boxes, formatted differently and including borders and shading:

    Goa, Bombay, Madras, New Delhi

9. On the *Packing* slide, insert a picture of clothing, copy it three times and create a design of the picture in four different sizes, e.g. slanted across the slide or arranged round the edge. Make sure all text is clearly visible.

10. Now apply a suitable design template and print a handout displaying all the slides before saving and closing.

 Module 6, sections 2.3 and 6.2

EXERCISES 5 AND 6

You will need to know how to:

▶ Customize design templates

Exercise 5 1. Reopen Nature.

2. Add a final slide that will have the title: Looking after the Environment.

3. Add text boxes to contain some of the following phrases: Collect up rubbish; Shut gates; Grow plants to attract insects; Keep away from nesting birds. (You may prefer to include your own choice of topics.)

4. Format the colour scheme to change the main background colour for this slide only, so that it stands out from the rest of the presentation but is still in the same style. If necessary, make changes to text colours so that they are still clearly visible.

5. Add a suitable image, e.g. a gate, bottle, rubbish bags, etc., either from the Clip Art gallery or drawn by hand, and give it a coloured border.

6. Print a handout displaying all the slides on one page.

7. Save the changes and close the file.

 Module 6, section 2.2

Exercise 6
1. Reopen **Holiday** and insert a second slide that includes text and pictures related to food and drink. Make sure the same design template is applied.

2. In Outline view, add the words **Food & Drink** to the list on the first slide.

3. In slide view, customize the background for this slide in different ways, e.g. by selecting different shades or colour combinations whilst staying with the same basic design.

4. Print a copy of the complete presentation and then update and close the file.

 Module 6, section 2.2

EXERCISES 7 AND 8

You will need to know how to:

▶ Use the Slide or Title Master to change your presentation

▶ Add footers and slide numbers

Exercise 7
1. Open **History**.

2. Apply a suitable design template to the presentation and customize it to your liking.

3. Using the Title Master, change the main title font on the title slide to Algerian. The title slide is not affected by altering the Slide Master, so you must alter the title slide manually or go to **View** > **Master** > **Title Master**.

4. Using the Slide Master, add a small WordArt object, **Time**, to every slide, positioned in the top, right-hand corner, and re-format all titles to Algerian.

5. Add slide numbers and the date as a footer.

6. Check that these objects appear on all the slides.

7. Go to the blank slide and change it to one with a numerical chart placeholder.

8. Add a main title – *Kings and Queens* – and then save and close the presentation.

 Module 6, section 2.4

Exercise 8 1. Open Transport.

2. Use the Slide Master to reformat the bullet points throughout your presentation.

3. Find a very small cartoon character illustrating a transport theme and add it to every slide.

4. Add your name in a very small font to the bottom left-hand corner of every slide.

5. Number all the slides.

6. Go to the Trains slide and, if necessary, change the slide layout to one that includes a placeholder for a bulleted list. Enter the following as a list headed by the subtitle **What You Will Need**:

   Tickets, Passport, Luggage, Reading matter and Guidebook

7. Position the following three WordArt objects on the Trains slide, angled and formatted to look different:

   Timetables; Across continents; Through the night

8. Check that the transport cartoon is still visible and print a copy of this slide only.

9. Update and close the presentation.

 Module 6, section 2.4

You will need to know how to:

▶ Create and format organization charts

Exercise 9 1. Open History and go to the slide with the organization chart placeholder.

2. Create the following chart with the title **Kings and Queens of England:**

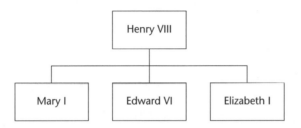

3. Save the amendments to the slide and then print one copy.

4. Now return to the chart and add the following descendants in a direct line from Mary: son **James I**, grandson **Charles I** and great grandsons **Charles II** and **James II**.

5. Add different borders and colours to the boxes.

6. Change the title font to bold and underlined and the names in the boxes to italic.

7. Save these changes and update the slide before printing a copy.

8. Close the file.

 Module 6, section 4.2

Exercise 10 1. Start a new presentation, select a blank slide layout or one with an organization chart placeholder and save the file as **Filing.**

2. Create an organization chart that shows the following:

Example of the Folders and Files
in my computer

My Documents
folder

Letters
folder

Health Club
folder

School
folder

6

3. Update your slide and print a copy.

4. Return to the chart and add the files as set out below:

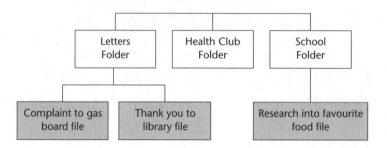

5. Make the folders yellow and the files green.

6. Change the title to: **A Folders and Files Hierarchy**

7. Reformat the text in your preferred style, and add borders or make any other changes you feel would improve the look of your chart.

8. Update your slide and print a copy of the amended chart.

9. Close the file.

 Module 6, section 4.2

EXERCISE 11

You will need to know how to:

♦ Add and format numerical charts

1. Open **History** and go to the slide with the numerical chart placeholder.

2. Insert a 2D column chart based on the following data and include titles for the main axes:

Monarch	Henry VII	Henry VIII	Edward	Mary	Elizabeth
Reign	24	38	6	5	45

3. Remove the legend and make sure the monarchs' names appear as x-axis labels.

4. Amend the slide title to read: Royal Reigns.

5. Print a copy of this slide alone.

6. Now change the chart type to a pie chart, add labels that show the years and include a legend.

7. On the slide, move both chart and main title higher up to make room for the following text:

   The average length of time on the throne in the 16th or 17th century was 21 years.

8. Save these changes and print a copy of the amended slide.

9. Close the file.

 Module 6, section 4.1

EXERCISE 12

You will need to know how to:

▸ Copy and resize objects

1. Open Transport and add a new blank slide.

2. Add the title: Sailing to France

3. Minimize your presentation.

4. Create the following spreadsheet using Excel or another spreadsheet package:

Dates	B and B	Standard Hotel	Premium Hotel
Nov–March	£219	£274	£374
March–May	£250	£305	£405
May–July	£280	£335	£490
Jul –Aug	£294	£349	£504
Sept	£250	£305	£405

6

5. Copy the data, and then minimize the spreadsheet package.

6. Paste the data on to your slide, and reposition and resize as necessary to display the data clearly.

7. Add the following text underneath the spreadsheet:

Cost of accommodation for 5 nights.

8. Print a copy of this slide only, and then save and close the presentation.

 Module 6, section 3.3

EXERCISES 13 AND 14

You will need to know how to:

▶ Add slide transitions

▶ Run a slide show automatically

▶ Hide slides during a slide show

Exercise 13 1. Create a new presentation to be called Cup of Tea (or choose a similar topic that can be set out in steps). Save as **Tea**.

2. Add the following five slides – feel free to vary the exact content of each slide – format backgrounds and borders and add images or WordArt where appropriate:

a) Slide 1: Title – How to make a cup of tea; subtitle – your name and the date.

b) Slide 2: Title – What you will need. List – tea leaves; teapot; kettle; water; spoon; cups and saucers; and possibly milk and sugar or slices of lemon.

c) Slide 3: Different types of tea, e.g. Earl Grey, Assam, Darjeeling, Green, and where tea comes from, e.g. India, Ceylon, China.

d) Slide 4: Title – Main Steps: shortened notes covering: Boil water; amount of tea in the pot – I spoonful per person; fill teapot with boiling water, leave 3 minutes (if preferred, have the milk ready in the cups), pour on the tea and add sugar/lemon.

e) Slide 5: Title – End Result – a refreshing cup of tea.

3. Run the presentation as a slide show and make any changes to slide order, pictures, design template, etc., if you think these are needed.

4. Run the show with slide 3 hidden.

5. Unhide this slide and run the show again.

6. Apply the same transition to all the slides and run the show. Change the type of transition until you are happy with it.

7. Now vary the transition for the first and/or last slide.

8. Update the presentation, and then print a six-slide handout page.

 Module 6, sections 5.2 and 6.3

Exercise 14 1. Open Transport.

2. Run the slide show and then add suitable backgrounds or apply an overall design template.

3. Change the slide order if necessary, and complete any slides that need extra text or images.

4. Set transitions for each slide and run the show automatically.

5. Make any changes to type and speed until you feel you have chosen the best combination of transitions.

6. Save the changes, print copies of any *two* slides only and then close the file.

 Module 6, sections 5.2 and 6.3

6

You will need to know how to:

▶ Animate slides

Exercise 15 1. Imagine you have been asked to give a talk on buying a house. You will need the following six slides:

Introduction (1)
Finding the right property (2)
Purchasing (3)
Moving in (4)
Gardening (5)
Conclusion (6)

2. Create an introductory first slide with the title of the talk, your name and a suitable picture. All the other slides should have a title taken from the above list.

3. On slide 2, add a bulleted list of different types of housing, e.g. bungalows, flats, semi-detached or detached houses, with a note about any pros and cons, e.g. no stairs, if this type of property is cheap or not, any gardens to maintain, the view, etc.

4. On slide 3, include the following data as a chart titled **Average Costs:**

Year	Solicitors	Surveyors	Banks
1980	£300	£80	£450
1990	£440	£186	£680
2000	£578	£245	£890

5. On slide 4, add suitable drawings or pictures to illustrate the topic, and include relevantly worded text boxes or WordArt objects, e.g. tiring, cups of tea, where's the dog? new neighbours, etc.

6. On slide 5, bullet points about gardens – where to buy plants, digging a pond, keeping the front tidy, weeding, etc., with illustrations.

7. On slide 6, summarize the contents of the talk and perhaps wish your audience good luck.

8. For each slide, experiment with animating objects and adding transitions.

9. Print a copy of all the slides, e.g. as a single handout or complete print-out. Save and close the presentation.

 Module 6, section 5.1

Exercise 16 1. Create a presentation (real or imaginary) about yourself that you will run as a slide show on the computer. You can include any aspect, e.g. family, home, work, leisure, pets, etc. (Naturally, if working with others, only disclose information you are happy to share.)

2. There should be six slides in the presentation which should include the following:

   a) an organization chart, e.g. showing a family tree, College staff or company management structure, etc.

   b) at least two examples of Clip Art and two of WordArt;

   c) one drawing produced either using the Drawing toolbar or within a separate drawing package;

   d) an overall colour scheme so that every slide has a similar 'look';

   e) transitions between slides;

   f) timing set so that the slides appear automatically;

   g) some pre-set animations.

3. Print the slides in the form of a single-page handout.

4. Save as Myself and close the file.

 Module 6, section 5.1

6

Information and communication

This final module tests your knowledge of the Internet. You need to be able to use a browser to visit Websites or search for information on the Word Wide Web, as well as store favourite Web page addresses. You will also need to be able to use an e-mail system to send and receive messages, attach files, maintain an address book and organize your messages in named folders.

Subjects covered in this section:

You will need to know how to:

▶ Use the browser navigation buttons

▶ Use URLs to open Web pages

▶ Use hyperlinks to open new pages

▶ Work with more than one application at a time

▶ Save files into folders

Exercise 1

1. Open your browser and connect to the Internet.

2. Note down the full URL of your home page, or copy it into a new Word document that you can save as **Web Addresses**.

3. Click a hyperlink text entry (it will probably be blue and underlined) to go to a new page. Make a note of the URL now showing in the address box and check the information on your screen. Finally open another page and note its URL and contents in the same way.

4. Return to your home page using the Back button.

5. Move backwards and forwards through the three pages you have opened and, if you can, find an image that you can click. Note the URL for the page that opens.

6. Type the following URL in the address box: www.bbc.co.uk and go to the BBC Website.

7. Use the index and hyperlinks on the page to find out the following:

   ● what the weather will be like in your nearest main town tomorrow;

   ● what is on television tonight;

   ● background information about a programme or personality of interest;

   ● how to contact someone at the BBC.

8. Close the browser window and disconnect if preferred.

 Module 7, sections 1.3 and 2.1

Exercise 2 1. You are going to find out what information is available on Websites created specifically for older Web surfers.

2. Open www.laterlife.com and use the index hyperlinks to explore their leisure pages, e.g. look at holidays, events, etc.

3. Repeat this activity on www.lifes4living.co.uk, www.50connect.com and www.retirement-matters.co.uk. Look particularly for leisure and travel information.

4. Close your browser.

5. You may like to think about which of the four sites you preferred and why.

 Module 7, sections 1.3 and 2.1

Exercise 3 1. Go to Tesco's main site, www.tesco.co.uk, and explore their index page. Click some of the hyperlinks to find out what the site has to offer.

2. Repeat this exercise by visiting two other supermarket sites – e.g. www.waitrose.com, www.safeway.co.uk or www.iceland.co.uk – and compare their attractiveness and ease of use.

3. Minimize your browser window (disconnect if you want to) and open a word-processing application.

4. Give three reasons why one of the sites you visited would be your favourite to recommend to first-time Web users wanting to find out about online shopping.

5. Give one reason why one of the sites was your least favourite.

6. Save the document as **Shops** into a new folder labelled **Web Research**.

7. Close the browser and disconnect if preferred.

 Module 7, sections 1.3 and 2.1

You will need to know how to:

▶ Use a directory

1. Connect to the Internet and open www.excite.com, www.yahoo.co.uk or any other directory site you have been recommended.

2. You are going to search for information on ice rinks in your area. Find a top-level category related to leisure or recreation and click it.

3. Find a sport and then ice skating sub-category and, in a new Word document, saved as **Skating**, note down the directory site and how many 'hits' (Websites listed) there are.

4. Search for any sites related to ice rinks – you may need to type the phrase into a search box.

5. Select two or three sites from the top five in the list and check if they identify a rink near you. If they do, make a note of the URL of the site in your Word document.

6. Now repeat the exercise using another directory and note the hits and useful sites.

7. Decide which was the best directory and which was the best Website for locating the information you were seeking and note their names in Skating.

 Module 7, section 3.1

EXERCISES 5 AND 6

You will need to know how to:

▶ Use a search engine for locating information

▶ Use key words

▶ Define search requirements

7

Exercise 5 1. Open www.google.com, www.altavista.com or any other search engine site recommended to you.

2. Type in *skating rinks.*

3. Note down the search engine you are using and number of 'hits' in your Skating file. The list should be far longer than when you used a directory.

4. Explore the top three sites on the list – do they provide useful information about local skating rinks?

5. Go back to the search engine page, add the word UK inside the query box and search again. Are the top three sites more relevant and useful?

6. Now put quotation marks round the phrase "*skating rinks*" and search again. How has the resultant list of sites changed?

7. Can you refine the search criteria even further? (Try using AND or +, or adding your county as well as UK.)

8. Now repeat the exercise using a different search engine and compare the results.

9. Finally, go to www.ask.co.uk and type in the question: Where is the nearest skating rink to [*add the name of your nearest main town*]? Decide if the results are better or worse than using key words.

10. In Skating, make a few notes about the success of your search, then save and close the file.

 Module 7, section 3.1

Exercise 6 1. Open your browser. You are going to find shops or garden centres in the UK where you can buy tropical fish and accessories for your aquarium.

2. Use a directory site to see if you can find the information using just the categories that are offered, e.g. leisure, pets, fish, etc. You do NOT want to locate sites for Aquariums and Sea Life Centres to visit.

3. Change to a second directory and follow their links to see if the information is easier to find on this site.

4. Open some of the Websites you are offered.

5. Use your **Back** button to return to the best Website and then type the full URL showing in the **Address** box into a new word processing document.

6. Underneath the URL, type: *this was the best site located for buying tropical fish that I found using* [*name of directory Website*] and save as Fish before minimizing the file.

7. Now go to a search engine Website and type **Aquariums** into the search box. Look at the types of site located by your search.

8. Use a variety of key words and search criteria – e.g. include UK, use NOT or AND, use + or –, or put some text in quotation marks, etc. – to narrow down the list to places in the UK where you can buy your aquarium requirements.

9. Visit several of the sites resulting from your search and then copy your preferred URL into Fish and type underneath: *this was the best site for buying fish located by using [name of search engine] and keying in [the key words you eventually used]*

10. Save and close the file and close your browser.

 Module 7, section 3.1

EXERCISE 7

You will need to know how to:

▶ Print a Web page

1. Use a variety of directories or search engines and experiment with key words or search criteria to locate the information below.

2. In all cases you may like to use a Word document for noting down the number of hits; whether the eventual site that had the information was one of the first five on a search list or was located further down the page; and if you encountered any problems during your search with any of the search engines.

   a) Find the names and addresses of three estate agents in your local area who sell flats. Go to the sites before noting down the details, to check that they are relevant (i.e. not selling commercial properties only, or out-of-date Websites, etc.).

   b) Now find a good UK site where you can buy fruit trees on-line.

   c) Discover the opening hours for either the Tate Modern in London or National Railway Museum in York.

   d) Finally, find out the price of a return ticket from Heathrow to Athens if you fly one day next month.

3. For each of the four searches, print *one* page from the Website that contains the most relevant information. Then close your browser.

 Module 7, section 3.3

7

You will need to know how to:

- Save a Web page

- Save an image from the Web

- Add a Web image to a document

---

1. In this exercise you will be sending a letter to a friend telling them about an area of mutual interest and using information you have found on the Web.

2. First locate some useful information about one of your hobbies, e.g. breeding goldfish, playing golf, collecting stamps, etc.

3. Save the most relevant Web page onto your computer or on disk as an HTML file where it should be saved into a new folder labelled **Web Information**. Give the file a name related to the hobby, e.g. **Golf1**.

4. Locate a relevant image and save it with a suitable name into a new folder labelled **Web Images**.

5. Go back to the first page you saved and then minimize the browser window, as you will need to return to the page to note its URL.

6. Open Word and write the following letter, first adding the address 43 Firtree Road, Beckwith, Derbyshire, DB5 1JT and today's date:

Dear Harvey

Searching the Web today I found the most brilliant information on [*name of hobby*]. The URL is [*full address of the Website*] but I've saved the information and will send it to you by e-mail once I get myself registered.

What do you think of this picture for our newsletter?

All the best

Jan

7. Now insert the image you saved into your document below the line **What do you think ...**, format and save the letter and print a copy.

8. Close Word and your browser.

 Module 7, section 3.1

You will need to know how to:

▶ Save a Web page as a text file

1. Use a directory or search engine to find a site offering you guidance on watercolour painting. You may like to include key words such as **tutorial** or **tips**.

2. Look at several of the sites resulting from your search and find the most helpful one.

3. Save the Web page as **Colour1** and print a copy.

4. Now save the page as a text file named **Colour2** and then close your browser.

5. Using Windows Explorer or the Desktop, locate the file **Colour2** and print a copy.

6. Compare the two printouts and then close all files.

 Module 7, section 3.1

You will need to know how to:

▶ Copy text from a Web page

▶ Copy images from a Web page

1. Go to a toyshop site – e.g. ToysRUs (www.toysrus.co.uk) or Hamleys (www.hamleys.co.uk) – and use the index or form provided on the site to find a doll that costs under £50. Then minimize your browser.

2. Open Word, start a new document and type the following:

   DOLLS FROM THE INTERNET

   There are many products you can find by using the Web. Here is a doll I found at [name of shop.]

3. Copy information about the product, including the price, from the Web page into your word-processed document. (It may appear as a table or in a different format.)

7

4. Return to the site and copy across a picture of the doll below the text in your document.

5. Save the document as Doll and print a copy.

6. Close your word processing application and browser.

 Module 7, section 3.1

EXERCISE 11

You will need to know how to:

‣ Bookmark a Web page (add to **Favorites** menu)

‣ Go to a bookmarked site

1. Return to the page you located on your hobby for Exercise 8 by typing the full URL into the **Address** box in your browser window.

2. So that it is quicker to return here in future, bookmark this site, changing the name if necessary to a shorter one. At this stage, do not choose any particular location for the bookmark, but just add it to your **Favorites** menu in the default position.

3. Try to find two other sites on a related topic – either click a hyperlink within the first site or use a search engine to locate them. In each case, bookmark the sites with relevant page names.

4. For one of these new sites, highlight the URL in the **Address** box and copy it into the clipboard.

5. Minimize the browser and open the letter you wrote in Exercise 8.

6. Add the following sentence to paragraph 1, paste in the URL copied to the clipboard and then update and close the file:

   There was also some useful information at [*address of one other site*] but not such good pictures.

7. Back in your browser, use your bookmark to go to the new site mentioned in your letter. Save the most useful page into your Web information folder with a name that distinguishes it from the first saved page, e.g. Golf2.

8. Close your browser.

 Module 7, section 2.2

You will need to know how to:

♦ Organize bookmarks

Exercise 12 1. Open your browser window, but work offline if preferred.

2. Open the **Favorites** menu and go to **Organize favorites**.

3. Create a new folder where you will store bookmarks to Websites about your hobby: label it suitably, e.g. **Golf**.

4. Locate and move two of your three bookmarked sites into this new folder.

5. Locate and delete the third bookmarked page.

6. Close **Favorites**.

7. Connect to the Internet, open the **Favorites** menu and use it to visit one of your hobby sites.

8. Click a hyperlink that you have not opened before and bookmark the new page you visit, adding it to your hobby folder.

9. Close your browser.

 Module 7, section 2.3

Exercise 13 1. Open your browser and find one newspaper Website, e.g. The *Guardian*, The *Observer*, The *Sunday Times*, The *Daily Mirror*, etc.

2. Bookmark the page and add it to a new **Favorites** folder you will create named **Newspapers**.

3. Find two more newspaper sites and add these to the **Newspapers** folder.

4. Now use a search engine to locate a weather report Website. Add this to a new **Weather** folder.

5. Finally, find a second weather Website but this time add it to the **Newspapers** folder.

6. Organize your bookmarks as follows:

a) Move the second weather Website bookmark out of the **Newspapers** folder and into the **Weather** folder.

b) Delete one of the three newspaper bookmarks.

c) Rename the **Newspaper** folder as **News**.

7

7. Use the **Favorites** menu to go to one newspaper Website.

8. Select the text of a short news report and copy it into a new word-processed document saved as **Paper**.

9. Copy an image from the page into the same document.

10. Print a copy of the document and update and close the file and your browser.

 Module 7, section 2.3

EXERCISE 14

You will need to know how to:

▶ Buy goods or services online

1. You have decided to buy a book as a present for a young nephew or niece. Go to an online book shop, e.g. www.amazon.co.uk; www.blackwells.co.uk or www.bol.co.uk

2. Search for **Alice in Wonderland** (if not available, find another well-known children's book, e.g. *Treasure Island* or *Just William*).

3. Follow the steps to add this book to your trolley or shopping cart and go through the process until you are asked to enter your credit card details. STOP at this point! (You may be asked to register with the site, but as this is free and could be useful for real purchases later, do so if you want to.)

4. Print a copy of the last page you reach that shows details of your proposed purchase.

5. Now go to any tour company site – e.g. www.markwarner.com, www.thomascook.co.uk or www.firstchoice.co.uk – and go through the process of buying any holiday, e.g. a one-week family holiday in Spain next month.

6. Check available accommodation/packages, select your preferred option and follow the purchasing procedure until asked for payment details.

7. Print a copy of the last page you reach that details the holiday you have chosen.

 Module 7, section 2.1

You will need to know how to:

◗ Open an e-mail system

◗ Compose and send an e-mail

Exercise 1

1. You are going to send an e-mail to John at Pearson Education.

2. Open your e-mail system and then the new message/composing box, staying offline if you can, and enter the following e-mail address: in the **To** box: john@pearsoned-ema.com

3. The subject of the message is Invitation to a Party.

4. Now type the following message in the main window:

   Hi John

   I have just moved house and want to invite you over for a house-warming party. Are you free next Saturday, 25th at 8.30?

   The address is 24 Mead Close, Warrington – just past the station on the left.

   Let me know if you can come. Hope to see you.

   Cheers

   [your first name]

5. Send your message, disconnect and close the e-mail system.

 Module 7, sections 4.3 and 5.3

Exercise 2

1. You are going to write to an imaginary television company commenting on a recent programme that you enjoyed or disliked.

2. In the **To** box enter the following TV company e-mail address: TVcomments@pearsoned-ema.com

3. The subject of the message is any real or imaginary programme title, e.g. Nine O-Clock News.

7

4. Write a short message mentioning something you enjoyed, or suggesting improvements. This is an example:

I am just writing to let you know that I am delighted to see that you now feature regional news quite strongly. In particular I am glad that the areas you cover have been reorganized so that people in the Berkshire/Oxfordshire area do not keep seeing repeats of London-based news items.

Many thanks for your excellent coverage.

[your name]

5. Send the message.

 Module 7, sections 4.3 and 5.3

EXERCISE 3

You will need to know how to:

▶ Use the spell-checker

▶ Set a priority on your message

1. You are going to send an e-mail to the Marketing Department at Pearson Education enquiring about books suitable for new computer owners.

2. If closed, open your e-mail system and then a new message window.

3. In the **To** box type: marketing@pearsoned-ema.com

4. The message subject is Computing for Beginners Books

5. Type the following message in the main window, RETAINING spelling mistakes to the words grateful and publications:

I would be gretful if you could send me the titles of 3 of your most recent pubblicatons that would be suitable for people like myself who have just bought a computer.

Many thanks

[Your name]

5. Now use the spell-checker to help you correct any mistakes.

6. Give your message a high priority.

7. Send the message.

 Module 7, section 5.3

You will need to know how to:

- Receive e-mails
- Reply to messages
- Forward messages
- Send copies
- Delete message text

Exercise 4

1. Open your Inbox and check that an automated response to your party invitation e-mail has arrived.

2. Open it and prepare the following reply:

    Hello John

    Glad to hear you can come. Vivien and I will look forward to showing you the new house. Wine to lubricate the proceedings will be gratefully received.

    Best wishes

    [Your name]

3. Delete your original message text showing in the main window.

4. Before sending, make sure you copy the reply to yasmin@pearsoned-ema.com and include a blind copy to yourself.

5. Forward a copy of the response you received to sarah@pearsoned-ema.com. Retain the original text and add this additional comment above it:

    Sarah

    Just heard John can come to my party. Are you free as well? You know where we live and it's on Saturday 25th at 8.30.

    Bye

    [Your name]

 Module 7, sections 5.2, 5.3 and 5.4

Exercise 5 1. Check your Inbox for an automated response from the message you sent in Exercise 17 to the Pearson Marketing Department.

2. Send the following reply, copying the message to yourself as a blind copy and leaving the original text in place as a reminder:

Thank you for the information you sent me. It will be most helpful.

With kind regards

[Your name]

3. Now forward the response from Marketing to John at Pearson Education, adding the following message:

As you were thinking of buying a computer I thought you might like the following information I have been sent by Marketing.

If you find out about any other books I might find useful, please let me know.

Best wishes

[Your name]

4. Check a little later to see if you have received the copy of your replies to John and Marketing that you sent yourself.

 Module 7, sections 5.2, 5.3 and 5.4

EXERCISES 6 AND 7

You will need to know how to:

▶ Print e-mails

▶ Copy text between messages or between applications

▶ Close messages without sending or saving (i.e. aborting e-mails)

Exercise 6 1. You have decided to send a late party invitation to Jack Spring.

2. Compose a new message with the Subject House Warming and enter the following e-mail address in the To box: jack.spring@webster.com

3. Open the original invitation you sent to John and copy the main text across into Jack's new message. Make sure you change John to Jack in the main message window.

4. Print a copy of the message and then cancel the e-mail.

 Module 7, sections 5.4 and 6.4

Exercise 7 1. Open your word processing application and create the following document:

Our house is on a new estate and can be quite confusing to find. Numbers 1 – 23 run parallel to Queen's Drive, but you have to turn right at the end of Charity Close before you start Numbers 24 – 42. Ours is the one with a red door and large conifer in the front garden.

2. Save as House and then minimize the file.

3. Open your e-mail system and compose a new message to Deidre Smith. Her e-mail address is d_smith@webster.com.

4. You are inviting her to tea next week. Enter the subject of the message as Tea and write the following:

Hello Deidre

So glad you can come over next Sunday.

5. Now restore your House document and copy the text across into the e-mail main message window.

6. Complete the message as follows:

Look forward to hearing about your holiday.

Best wishes

[your name]

7. Print a copy of the message and then close without saving.

 Module 7, sections 5.4 and 6.4

EXERCISE 8

You will need to know how to:

- Add e-mail details to an address book
- Insert addresses automatically into new messages
- Save messages in draft format

1. A number of examination bodies have Websites and offer an e-mail information service.

2. Add the e-mail addresses of the following three such organizations to your Address Book:

7

- City and Guilds: 1 Giltspur Street, London EC1A 9DD; enquiry@cityandguilds.com

- Oxford Cambridge and RSA Examinations (OCR): tel.: 01223 553998; helpdesk@ocr.org.uk

- Edexcel: tel.: 0870 240 9800; enquiries@edexcel.org.uk

3. Add the other information provided in appropriate places within your Address Book.

4. Open a new message window and automatically insert the e-mail address for OCR stored in your Address Book into the **To** box.

5. Type the following message:

   I am interested in taking a City and Guilds Business studies course next year. Please would you send me details of Centres where I could study the subject locally.

6. Add the subject of the message: Business studies courses in (*your county or main town*).

7. Save the message in your Drafts folder.

8. Close and then re-open your e-mail system. Open your draft message to OCR and amend it to read:

   ... taking an OCR Business studies course ...

9. Now print a copy of the message, save the changes and then close so that it remains in your Drafts folder.

 Module 7, sections 6.1, 6.2 and 6.4

You will need to know how to:

▶ Create a group e-mail address

▶ Send messages to everyone on a mailing list

▶ Delete an address

▶ Edit an address

1. You have entered the City and Guilds e-mail address incorrectly. Open your e-mail system and Address Book and change it to: **enquiry@city-and-guilds.co.uk**

2. Add the following e-mail addresses to your Address Book:

   ● The British Tourist Authority: **enquiries@bta.org.uk**

   ● The Heart of England Tourist Board: **htinfo@bta.org.uk**

3. Create a group e-mail address labelled **Tourist Boards** and add the Heart of England Tourist Board and BTA addresses.

4. Now create a group e-mail address labelled **Exam Bodies** to include City and Guilds, Edexcel and OCR. Add to it the e-mail address for the British Computer Society (**bcshq@bcs.org.uk**), which should *not* have its own entry in your Address Book.

5. Compose the following message to **Exam Bodies** with the subject **IT Training** and print a copy:

   Do you offer any qualifications in IT training for people who have an ECDL certificate? If so, please would you send me details.

   Many thanks

   [Your name].

6. Save the message into your **Drafts** folder.

7. Finally, locate and delete the individual entry for **Edexcel** in your Address Book.

 Module 7, section 6.2

EXERCISE 10

You will need to know how to:

▶ Restore deleted messages

▶ Mark messages as unread

1. Imagine you are writing from an advertising company, *Selling UK*. You are going to send the following message to John at Pearson Education.

2. The subject of the message is **Distance Learning Advertisement**.

3. This is the message:

   John

   It was good to meet you last week. I have had a think about the campaign and want to confirm my view that we should take a more negative approach. Negative campaigning is the IN thing, and I'm sure we will sell far more courses if we drop the final part of your presentation.

   Do you still disagree?

   Look forward to your views.

4. Add the following:

   Jay McWhortle
   Managing Director and Campaign Designer
   Selling UK
   Tel: 0108 4321000
   http://www.sellinguk.co.uk

5. Send the message with a copy to yourself.

6. When the copy arrives, read it and then mark it as unread.

7. Delete the message.

8. Open the **Deleted Items** folder, locate and restore the copy, and return it to your **Inbox**.

 Module 7, sections 5.1 and 6.3

You will need to know how to:

◗ Attach files to e-mail messages

Exercise 11 1. Open a word processing application and create the following document:

From: Head Office

To: All Heads of Department

Date: (today's)

Subject: Car Parks

You will be glad to learn that the new car park is now available alongside Block D. Any member of staff who would like to use it should complete the tear-off slip at the bottom of this memo and send it to Security. I hope this will put an end to lateness of staff due to car parking difficulties in the City.

....

To: Security

From: ....   Department: ....

Please issue me with a car sticker so that I can use the new car park. My car

registration number is ....

Signed ....

Date ....

2. Save as Car Parking and close the file.

3. Now open your e-mail system and write the following message to send to Yasmin at Pearson Education. Copy it to Sarah with a blind copy to yourself. The subject is Parking.

Dear Colleagues

I have just received the attached memo from HQ. Please print out and reply so that we can sort out this wretched parking problem once and for all.

Deirdre Wessex
Head of Finance

4. Attach the document Car Parking and print a copy of the message showing the contents of the attachment box.

5. Send the message.

 Module 7, section 5.3

Exercise 12 **1.** John at Pearson Education wants to find out more about the ECDL.

2. Write the following e-mail. The subject of the message is **Computer Training**.

ECDL covers seven aspects of computers: general theory about its use; filing and file management; word processing, databases; spreadsheets; presentations and the Internet. You can take the modules in any order and eventually will receive a certificate recognized world-wide.

3. Copy the text into a new word processed document, save as **ECDL text** and then close the file.

4. Back in your message, attach the file **ECDL text** to your e-mail. Now add the following text to your message:

I attach a copy of my words to check that attaching files is working properly.

5. Send the message with the attachment.

 Module 7, section 5.3

Exercise 13

You will need to know how to:

▶ Open attachments

▶ Delete attachments

---

1. Start a new Word document and insert a picture of a car, e.g. from Clip Art. Save as **Car Picture** and close the file.

2. Check your e-mail system and when the response to your parking message sent in Exercise 25 arrives in your Inbox, open the attachment and complete the reply slip with the following information:

Name: David Holmes

Department: Arts and Media

Car registration number: V980 MUI

3. Save the amended document as **My Car** and print a copy before closing the file.

4. Now open a new message window addressed to yourself and write the following message that has the subject **Car Park Permit**:

   Dear Security Officer Biggins

   Just in case the internal post plays up again, I am e-mailing my car details so that my parking permit can be forwarded as soon as possible.

   Many thanks

   Dave

5. Attach both the My Car and Car Picture files and save the message in your drafts folder.

6. Print a copy of the message showing the attachments in the attachment box.

7. Now delete the Car Picture attachment and send the message.

8. When it arrives in your Inbox, check that only one file is attached.

 Module 7, section 5.4

EXERCISE 14

You will need to know how to:

♦ Create folders for storing messages

♦ Copy, move or delete messages

1. Open your e-mail system and Inbox.

2. Create a subfolder within the Inbox folder labelled In-Exercises.

3. Move at least three of the messages you have received working through this section into the folder.

4. Locate and delete the Selling UK message.

5. Now create a subfolder within your Sent Messages folder labelled Out-Exercises and move at least two messages you have sent into it.

6. Find a third message and save a copy into your new folder.

7. Delete the reply you sent to Marketing thanking them for their information, and check that it is in the **Deleted Items** folder.

 Module 7, section 6.3

7

You will need to know how to:

▶ Sort messages

▶ Find messages

1. Open your Inbox and sort the messages in date order – the most recent messages at the top. Repeat the sort so the messages are in the opposite order.

2. Now open the Sent folder and sort messages by subject in alphabetical order.

3. Using the Find facility, locate the message to the OCR concerning Business studies courses, making sure you look in all your folders. When it has been located, move it to the **Deleted items** folder.

4. Address a new message to yourself and then find all your messages to John at Pearson Education. Open two different messages and copy the main text into your new message window. Add the following text at the top of the message:

   The following text was sent to John in 2 different messages.

5. Send the message.

6. When it arrives in your Inbox, print a copy, and then delete the message and close your e-mail system.

 Module 7, section 6.3

Test your information and communication knowledge with this crossword.

ACROSS

1 Part of a Web page (5)

3 If you see this, you are over a hyperlink (4)

6, 14 Go here to save telephone charges (3, 4)

8 Needed to use the Internet (5)

10 Connects two Web pages (4)

12 Abbreviation for all those pages (3)

13 Starting page (4)

15 The Web address (3)

16 Box showing where your files are (6)

19 Keep the address handy (8)

20 Who are you? (2)

21 Click this to return (4)

22 Start the search (2)

23 Talking over the Internet (4)

28 Using technology to communicate (3)

29, 40 Help you find information (6, 6)

30 Do this to start searching (7)

31 Nasty germ (5)

32 Well known search engine (9)

35 Get rid of something (6)

41 Do this if downloading is too slow (4)

42 Example of a directory (5)

44 Post an e-mail (4)

46 Words to type in before searching (3)

47 Important consideration when buying on the Internet (8)

48 Needed to view Web pages (7)

DOWN

2 Do this to reload the page (7)

3 Code (4)

4 Send it to someone else (7)

5 Move through the list (6)

7 Place to revisit (8)

9 List of what's on the site (5)

11 It appears when you reply (2)

17 Sort things out (8)

18 Useful Website (6)

20 Use it for information and communication (8)

24 Results of a search (4)

25 @ (2)

26 Your machine may be one (2)

27 The opposite of 6 Across (6)

29 New sport (7)

33 Send files with your message (6)

34 Keep your friends safely stored here (7,4)

36 See stars when you type this (8)

37 Hundreds of multimedia documents (3)

38 Unwanted mail (4)

39 Make one to keep things tidy (6)

43 Visit the sites and view the details (6)

45 Could be a hard one (4)

2

Model answers

This part of the book contains model answers that show you what your finished work might look like, or what you should see on screen if you have performed the tasks correctly. Although your answers and computer screens may be quite different from the following examples, these will give you an idea of what you should be aiming for.

Part 2 is also broken down into sections that relate to each of the seven ECDL modules:

Module number

1. Concepts of information technology
2. Using the computer and managing files
3. Word processing
4. Spreadsheets
5. Databases
6. Presentation
7. Information and communication

Concepts of information technology

ANSWERS TO INTRODUCTORY QUESTIONS

1. You might mention Microsoft Publisher™ and explain that it is used to produce publications such as brochures, business cards or leaflets.

2. Networked computers can share expensive hardware such as printers; can share files so that different departments can access the same information; and can encourage collaborative working, e.g. contributing different information that will be brought together in a single publication.

3. Passwords prevent unauthorized people from accessing computer systems or stored information such as personnel records. The ***** stop people seeing your password if they are standing close to you when you type it in.

4. You could have mentioned any of the following ways that hospitals might use computers: to store patient information such as names and addresses, contact numbers, etc.; to keep details of a patient's medical history and current medication; a national database to help hospitals find empty beds; and a register of donors for organ transplants. In addition, computers are used for medical research.

5. You need to be aware that computer files can be lost or corrupted so that keeping backups means you will always have a reasonably recent copy of the information.

6. Viruses are commonly transferred by e-mail or when downloading programs from the Internet, or from using an infected floppy diskette. Safety measures include installing and regularly updating anti-virus software, and never installing programs or borrowing disks from an unknown source.

7. This Act is your safeguard against other people using your private information stored on computer. Organizations keeping personal records must be registered and abide by the law. Banks may hold your current or deposit

account details or information on loans; a school or college will have your personal contact details and information on qualifications; and a doctor will keep your full medical history.

8. System software, such as the operating system of your computer, is needed to maintain the efficient operation of your computer or peripherals such as printers. Application software allows you to perform specific tasks, e.g. word processors enable you to write letters, and browsers allow you to view Web pages.

9. The Internet is the name given to the networks of computers that are linked around the world and that enable you to send information from one computer to another. The World Wide Web is made up of thousands of multimedia pages containing text, pictures, sounds and moving images that are stored on computers and that each have a unique address, the URL. This allows you to locate any page and download it on to your computer.

10. GUI stands for Graphical User Interface and is easy to use as you work from menus and labelled buttons rather than having to type in code, and can have several applications running inside windows that are open on screen at the same time.

11. The telephone system allows you to speak to someone, or send fax, e-mail or telex messages. All except e-mail can be used without a computer.

12. You normally find a floppy diskette in the A: drive, the hard disk in the C: drive, and CD-ROM disks in the D: drive.

13. Systems development usually involves research, analysis, programming, and then testing and implementation. The programmer is involved in writing the software and documentation for the system.

14. E-commerce is the use of the Internet for business. Shopping online can save time as you won't need to visit a shop, save effort in carrying goods home and allows you to find the cheapest items, as you can compare prices very easily from your home. Disadvantages include not being able to see and handle the goods, it is difficult to take advantage of special offers that may be very local to an individual outlet, and the system may breakdown and prevent you placing your order.

15. Storing copies of files on floppy diskettes means you will still have your work even if something happens to the originals on the computer. You can also carry floppy diskettes around so that you can easily transfer files to different machines.

ANSWERS TO ADVANCED QUESTIONS

1. Working safely with a computer should involve taking regular breaks, sitting in a chair that encourages a good posture, keeping everything within easy reach to avoid stretching, cutting down on glare from the screen, holding the mouse lightly and supporting wrists with a wrist rest.

2. The CPU is the central processing unit and is the 'brains' of your computer as it determines everything it does. Its speed is measured in megahertz (MHz).

3. Customers are able to view statements and details of recent transactions in any of their bank accounts; they can pay bills by transferring money electronically to another account; and they can transfer money between accounts, such as current and savings accounts, held with the same bank.

4. Laser printers work by building up an image on an electrically charged drum. Pigment-loaded resin is attracted to the charged areas and heat is then used to melt and bond the resin to paper. Inkjet printers spray droplets of ink onto the paper from rows of nozzles.

5. The advantages of e-mail include no need to use stamps or go to the postbox, sending messages across the world very quickly, and being able to send large numbers of messages for the cost of a local phonecall.

6. Unlike ClipArt, pictures with © next to them are not free for you to use, and the copyright symbol is there to protect the rights of the owner. You must seek permission from the artist or photographer who created them before you can copy or use them, e.g. for cards or in publications.

7. Portable computers are called laptops or notebooks. They use batteries rather than mains power, have a built-in pointing device such as a touch pad, and have flat, liquid-crystal display screens inside the case.

8. Input devices include mouse, keyboard, scanner, digital camera and microphone. Output devices are monitor, speakers and printers. Printers are described in answer 19, so you might describe how the mouse works. It contains a ball that is free to roll. As the mouse is moved over a flat surface the ball rotates, and sensors send digital information to the computer regarding its position. This is translated into an arrow or other shape that moves around the screen.

9. RAM stands for Random Access Memory. It differs from ROM as it is lost when the computer is turned off, and it can have new data written into it.

10. Formatting a floppy diskette involves organizing the magnetic material into tracks and sectors that have a unique address, so that information stored there can be located easily. The answer to formatting a hard disk is (c) – only on special occasions. This is because formatting destroys all the information stored on the disk, and the hard disk houses important information such as your application software and files.

11. Shareware is the term applied to versions of software such as desktop publishing or zipping programs that are made available on the Internet and can be downloaded and used without an initial purchase. They normally have an expiry date, after which you must send a small fee to the program author. They differ from freeware, as these programs are entirely free to use.

12. Pointing devices are input devices that usually control an arrow used in GUI systems to select the menus and icons and carry out tasks such as moving text. You may come across joysticks, touch screens, track balls, mice or light pens. Mice have been described in answer 23, but touch screens are different as users use a finger to touch the screen when they want to choose from a series of options.

13. A modem is needed if you want to communicate with other computers on a network that uses the telephone cable system, such as the Internet. A modem (the name stands for *modulator–demodulator*) converts the digital information used by your computer into an analogue signal that can be sent down a telephone cable. The current top speed of a modem is 56kbps.

14. Zipping is the process of compressing large files so that they take up far less space.

15. Hard disks are usually measured in GB, but RAM, CD-ROMs and floppy diskettes are all measured in MB.

2

Using the computer and managing files

ANSWERS TO INTRODUCTORY QUESTIONS

1. To shut down properly, click the **Start** button, select **Shut Down** and check the *Shut down* option before clicking **OK**. You must do this so that temporary files or unsaved work are organized properly before your next session.

2. a) Image files may be bitmap (BMP), jpeg (JPG) or gif (GIF)
    b) Text files are .txt, Web pages are .htm, Excel spreadsheets are .xls and Word documents are .doc.

3. My **Help** menu indicated that you can open the calculator by clicking **Start**, then choosing **Programs**, **Accessories**, and finally **Calculator**.

4. To resize a window, first click its **Restore** button, then move the mouse pointer over any boundary and drag the edge in or out with the two-way arrow that will be displayed.

5. To find your default printer, you can select **Start | Settings | Printers** and check which icon has a tick above it. To change the default, click an alternative printer icon and go to **File | Set as default**.

6. Try holding down **Ctrl** and **Alt** and then clicking **Delete** to unfreeze a computer. In the window that appears, click **End Task**. You can repeat pressing **Ctrl + Alt + Delete** to restart the computer completely, or follow the shut down procedure described in answer 1, but check **Restart** in the Shut down window.

7. I am working with a computer operating Windows 98 on an AMD-K6™ 3D processor, with 128MB RAM

8. My Recycle Bin shows the following details:

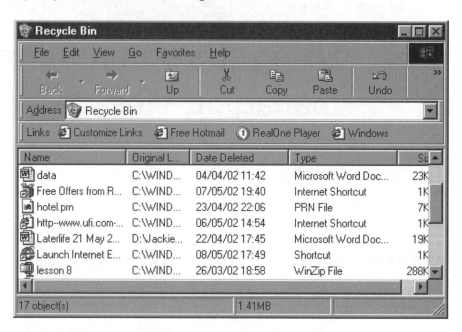

9. My search located six files or folders, shown below.

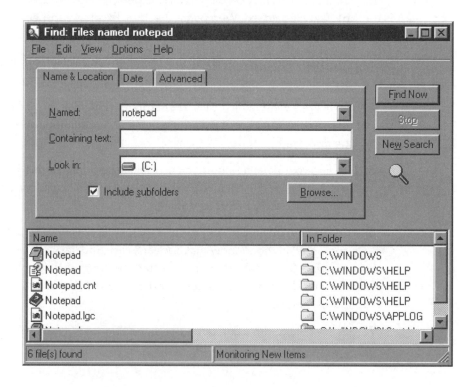

10. The steps are as follows:
    1. Open a zipping program such as Winzip
    2. Create an archive in which to compress the files by clicking **New**. Save and name this as normal.
    3. Browse your files and click by name any that you want to compress. Then click **Add**. The files will appear in the archive window.
    4. Close the archive and treat it just like a normal file.

ANSWERS TO EXERCISES

Exercise 1   Creating new folders on the desktop.

Exercise 2   Changing the name of the folder Veg to Vegetables.

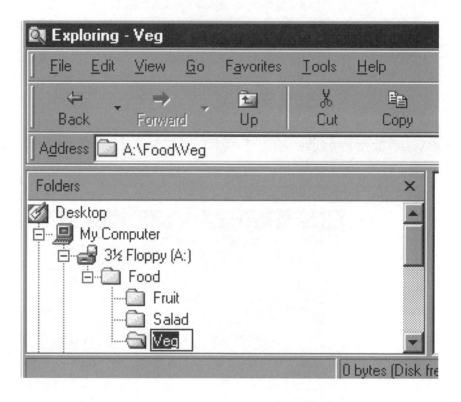

Exercise 3   Deleting a file should result in a request for confirmation.

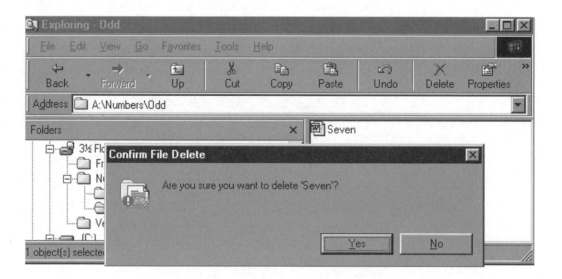

Exercise 4   Moving files in Windows Explorer.

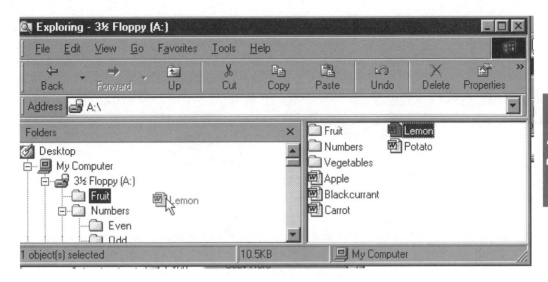

Exercise 6   Finding the details for 'Potato'. (Exercise 5 will produce a similar result.)

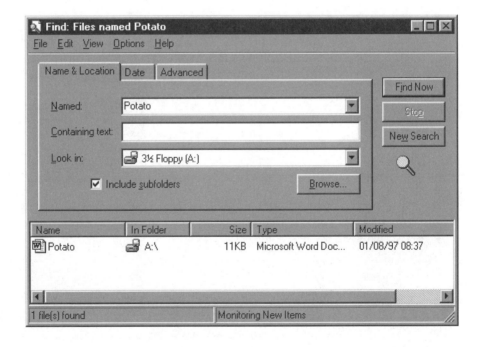

Moving more than one file at the same time.

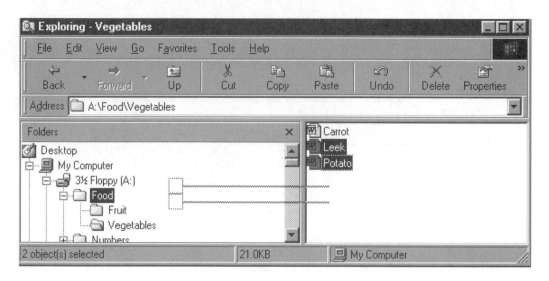

Exercise 7   Saving a file into a named folder. (Exercise 8 will produce a similar result.)

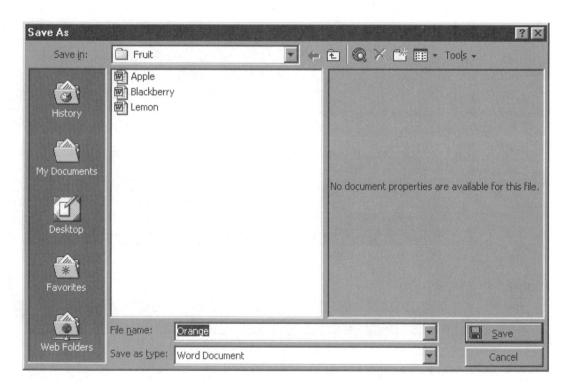

Exercise 9   Showing the contents of a folder.

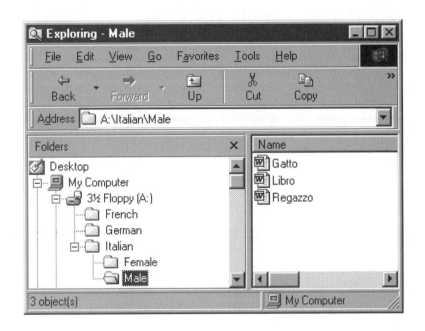

Word processing

ANSWERS TO INTRODUCTORY EXERCISES

Exercise 1   SURFACE FEEDERS

All the fish found 'just under the surface' have a perfectly straight back, which allows their upturned mouths (ideal for scooping up floating foods, usually insects) to get right up to the surface. Foods which float for some time are ideal for these fish.

A common surface feeder is the Zebra Danio. This fish is a native of India and is very active and lively. It can reach a size of about 5 cm and is best kept in shoals.

[My Name]

Exercise 2   THE POTENTIAL OF MUSIC

Teachers generally provide a stimulating environment for children in their classes, with respect to sight and touch. Other experiences may be overlooked. One of the senses which can be educated quite easily is hearing. Sounds are all around us in the infants and with careful structuring they can even become organized sounds – music.

Children make sounds all the time – they talk, shout, cry, scream or sing. A good way to focus on sounds is to use rhymes and poems and to tell stories needing 'sound effects', such as those of police cars, ambulances, trains or ghosts.

[My Name]

Exercise 3   FIGHTING FISH

All the fish found 'just under the surface' have a perfectly straight back, which allows their upturned mouths (ideal for scooping up floating foods, usually insects) to get right up to the surface. Foods which float for some time are ideal for these fish.

A common surface feeder is the Zebra Danio. This fish is a native of India and is very active and lively. It can reach a size of about 5 cm and is best kept in shoals.

The Siamese Fighting Fish is hardy, but you can only have one male in a tank otherwise fighting will break out. If you want to see it display, put a mirror at the side of the tank. Aquarium-cultivated strains usually have bodies and fins of one colour, apart from the Cambodia Fighter that has a cream body and coloured fins.

[My Name]

MUSIC GAMES

Teachers generally provide a stimulating environment for children in their classes, with respect to sight and touch. Other experiences may be overlooked. One of the senses which can be educated quite easily is hearing. Sounds are all around us in the infants and with careful structuring they can even become organized sounds – music.

Children make sounds all the time – they talk, shout, cry, scream or sing. A good way to focus on sounds is to use rhymes and poems and to tell stories needing 'sound effects', such as those of police cars, ambulances, trains or ghosts.

One activity teachers can try is to sit the group in a circle. Everyone claps three times, then leaves a space equivalent to three more claps, and then everyone claps three times again. How the gap is filled is up to the teacher, but you could alternate between 'oohs' and 'aahs'.

[My Name]

Exercise 4   The Problems of Heart Disease

Heart disease causes a quarter of all deaths in Britain. It is the biggest killer of middle-aged men in the developed world.

You need a healthy heart to pump blood around your body, and heart muscle needs food and oxygen for it to keep contracting. These are carried in the coronary arteries. If the arteries get blocked, then it can cause heart disease.

The artery wall can become rough and this can cause the blood to clot and block the vessel. A total blockage or thrombosis can cause a heart attack. Here the supply of oxygen is cut off, there are severe pains in the chest and the affected part of the heart is damaged.

Exercise 5   Using the spell-checker:

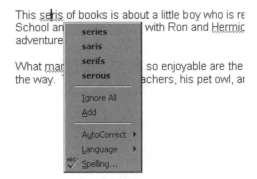

Harry Potter – Uncorrected

This seris of books is about a little boy who is re
School an [series] with Ron and Hermic
adventure [saris]
            [serifs]
What mar [serous] so enjoyable are the
the way. ...achers, his pet owl, an

Ignore All
Add

AutoCorrect ▸
Language ▸
Spelling...

Exercise 6   ## The Problems of Heart Disease

Heart disease causes a quarter of all deaths in Britain. It is the biggest killer of middle-aged men in the developed world.

You need a healthy heart to pump blood around your body, and heart muscle needs food and oxygen for it to keep contracting. These are carried in the coronary arteries. If the arteries get blocked, then it can cause heart disease.

The artery wall can become rough and this can cause the blood to clot and block the vessel. A total blockage or thrombosis can cause a heart attack. Here the supply of oxygen is cut off, there are severe pains in the chest and the affected part of the heart is damaged.

<u>You can take care of your heart by eating more poultry and fish. Cut down on fried foods and red meat and always eat plenty of fruit and vegetables.</u>

Exercise 7   ## ONE POT WONDER
(Serves 2–3)

4 lamb chops
700g peeled and diced carrots, potatoes and swedes
pinch of dried oregano
15ml tomato puree

Preheat the oven to gas mark 7. Tip vegetables into a shallow ovenproof dish and arrange the lamb chops over the top. Sprinkle over the herbs, season then roast in the oven for 15 minutes.

Mix the tomato puree with a cupful of hot water and pour over the chops and vegetables. Continue cooking for another 20 minutes.

Exercise 8   15 October 2002

Breakfast at Hotel Belle Vue

fruit juice or cereal

++++++

fried egg, sausage, bacon, fried tomatoes, fried bread

+++++++++

grilled kippers

++++++++

toast and marmalade

+++++++++

tea, hot chocolate or coffee.

Breakfast will be served from 7.30–9.00 a.m. Please note that some items on the menu may change according to availability as we like to offer the freshest ingredients in our meals.

Exercise 9   # Catching the Fever

Viruses are an unpleasant fact of computing life we could all do without. However, by being aware of the nature of the problem you can guard against the risk of PC infections.

If you've yet to be infected by a computer virus, you're in a dwindling minority. There are now so many viruses in circulation that it's almost impossible to use a PC for any length of time and not encounter one. Cutting through the hype about viruses isn't easy though, particularly when some computer users add to it by forwarding bogus virus alerts to all and sundry.

15/10/2002

Exercise 10   IT'S <u>OK</u> TO GIVE ORDERS

Good behaviour in children is required not as a whim of parents but to make practical living easier. Unlike parents of the Victorian era, we do not need pointless obedience, such as brushing one's hair before tea, but we do ask children to co-operate to make life easier.

When children don't co-operate, the parents find their life inconvenienced. Soft parents will soon find they are being given the run-around. However much they want to give in and not inhibit their children's creativity, these parents find they are very angry and tired of the troubles this causes, and attempt to restore order. Feeling steamed up, they may lash out and discipline their children in a way that they and the child know is somewhat out of control. This is bad for everyone concerned and there are more successful ways to give orders.

Be clear in your own mind: It's not a request or open to debate, it's a demand which you have a right to make.

Make good contact: Stop what you are doing, go up close to the child and get her to look at you.

Be direct: Say, "I want you to ... now. Do you understand?" Make sure you get a "yes" or "no" answer.

3

Exercise 11

Mr & Mrs S.M. Tyler
Green Acres
17 Bathurst Close
Bath, Avon
BT3 7PY

The Editor
Greenfingers Magazine
44 Old Station Yard
Kingley
Wellington
WT5 7LL

22 May 2002

Dear Sir

Early Hellebores

You may like to know that I followed the advice in last month's edition of your magazine and ordered 26 Hellebores.

When they arrived, they were planted under a fir tree at the bottom of the garden, which you indicated in your article was an ideal spot.

According to your column, the plants would flower profusely from January until late April, and would give my garden much needed colour at this damp and dank time of year.

Unfortunately, I have wasted £35!

Only three of the plants have flowered, and these were a sickly sight. The rest provided a feeble show of leaf and then gave up and dropped all their foliage.

Frost damage was clearly visible on many of the plants and they obviously needed far more light and water.

I am very disappointed at the poor advice I received and have cancelled my subscription to your magazine forthwith.

Yours with regret

S. M. Tyler

Exercise 12

Come to a *House Warming* Party!

Jane & Rick

Invite .... to their

House Warming

at

12 Rymans Road, Reading

on

Saturday, 22 June

Exercise 13   15 October 2002

Breakfast at Hotel Belle Vue

fruit juice or stewed prunes

(choice of tomato, orange or pineapple juice)

++++++

Porridge, Muesli or Cornflakes

+++++

grilled kippers

+++++

*fried, boiled or scrambled egg, sausage, bacon, fried tomatoes,
fried bread*

+++++++

toast and marmalade

++++++++

tea, hot chocolate or coffee.

Breakfast at Hotel Belle Vue

Breakfast will be served from 7.30 – 9.00 a.m. Please note that some items on the menu may change according to availability as we like to offer the freshest ingredients in our meals.

Exercise 14   15/10/2002

THE VERY BEST OF FRANCE

1. <u>**Normandy:**</u>
   - alluring medieval villages,
   - upmarket 19th-century seaside resorts,
   - the island-abbey of Mont St Michael
   - endless windswept beaches on the Cotentin peninsula.

2. <u>**Brittany:**</u>
   - magnificent beaches lining the north coast,
   - dramatically wind-battered west coast,
   - gentler bays in the south
   - rolling countryside inland.

3. <u>**Burgundy:**</u>
   - a wealthy region of forests, meadows, magnificent ancient cities
   - some of the world's great vineyards.

   4. <u>**The Alps:**</u>
      - holidays in the mountains,
      - less crowded than the Mediterranean coast,
      - ski lifts to take you up to the peaks for long hikes
      - après-ski haunts for morning coffee.

Plumbing

Living in a flat means plumbing and drainage emergencies can cause problems above and beyond those experienced by house owners. After all, leaking water wherever it comes from won't just cause damage to your own property. It can also cause considerable distress to neighbours and can have potentially disastrous results if you are away for a while.

Here are some of the emergencies that can happen to flat owners:

- Burst pipes
- Leaking washing machine
- Nail through heating pipe
- Blocked kitchen sink
- Blocked toilet
- Leaking radiator valve

Views

However, there are also great advantages to flats. For example, if you are on a fifth floor or above, the views can be fantastic, and burglars are less likely to carry your heavy furniture or electric goods down many flights of stairs or in full view of other residents if they are brazen enough to use the lifts. This makes flats a good choice for those who are away for a good part of their working day.

3

ANSWERS TO ADVANCED EXERCISES

Exercise 1   Inserting a page break:

Printing current page only:

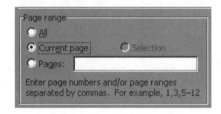

Using headers:

Exercise 2   Page 1 should look as shown below:

<u>Watercolour Painting</u>

Size

The size of a painting is very much a matter of personal preference. There are no rules, but if working small, say 6 × 4in., gives you confidence, that's fine. On the other hand, it can be exciting to work large and it can increase your enthusiasm. If you ever feel you are getting stale or need a change, try working in a different size and you might be amazed at the different work you create.

Page 2 showing footer at bottom of page 1:

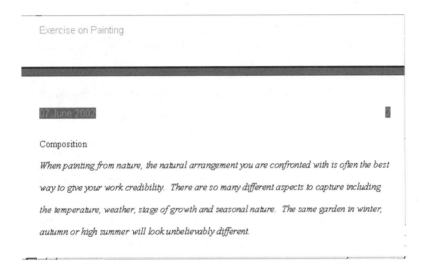

Exercise on Painting

07 June 2002   2

Composition

When painting from nature, the natural arrangement you are confronted with is often the best way to give your work credibility. There are so many different aspects to capture including the temperature, weather, stage of growth and seasonal nature. The same garden in winter, autumn or high summer will look unbelievably different.

Exercise 3

<u>Special Characters</u>

Word processing packages often allow you to use symbols or special characters to liven up your documents.

A good use for these pictorial symbols is for children's games. For example, if you typed a message in a normal font and then applied Wingdings to the text, it would be impossible to read. Offering the alphabet code for each symbol would then allow a child to decipher the message. You should be able to find a book 📖, telephone, ☎, pair of scissors ✂ or smiley face ☺ when using Wingdings fonts, or insert symbols for hearts ♥, diamonds ♦, spades ♠ and clubs ♣ when searching the gallery of Symbols.

Exercise 4

FOR SALE

Flat 49, Seaview Road, Southbourne

Estate Agents: Grimble & Denton, estate agents of 22 Wattis Road, Boscombe, Bournemouth BN5 2AA.

Price: £250,000

Summary: A beautifully appointed ground floor 3-bed property with excellent sea views and balcony, situated close to the picturesque beaches of Southbourne. Included in the price are fitted cupboards, electric hob, carpets and barbecue. There is a garage behind the property which is in a well-kept block built around 1950. Internal inspection highly recommended.

Hall: Carpet, entryphone, radiator.

Sitting room: Large French windows to balcony, seaviews, fireplace, radiator, TV point, telephone point, shelving, Venetian blinds.

Dining Room: Wood floor, radiator, window to rear.

Bedroom 1: Seaviews, fitted cupboards, carpet, radiator.

Bedroom 2: Window to rear, radiator.

Bedroom 3: Window to side, fitted cupboards, radiator.

Kitchen: Breakfast bar, tiled floor, fitted cupboards, sink unit, electric hob, wall-mounted electric oven, plumbing for washing machine, door to communal gardens.

Bathroom: Gold taps, shower unit, green suite, glazed window to rear.

Study: Glass chandelier, wooden floor.

Exercise 5   The estate agent's property description using Clip Art:

<u>FOR SALE</u>

Flat 49, Seaview Road, Southbourne

Estate Agents: Grimble & Denton, estate agents of 22 Wattis Road, Boscombe, Bournemouth BN5 2AA.

Price: £250,000

Summary: A beautifully appointed ground floor 3-bed property with excellent sea views and balcony, situated close to the picturesque beaches of Southbourne. Included in the price are fitted cupboards, electric hob, carpets and barbecue. There is a garage behind the property which is in a well-kept block built around 1950. Internal inspection highly recommended.

Hall: Carpet, entryphone, radiator

Sitting room: Large French windows to balcony, seaviews, fireplace, radiator, TV point, telephone point, shelving, Venetian blinds.

Dining Room: Wood floor, radiator, window to rear.

Bedroom 1: Seaviews, fitted cupboards, carpet, radiator

Bedroom 2: Window to rear, radiator

Bedroom 3: Window to side, fitted cupboards, radiator

Kitchen: Breakfast bar, tiled floor, fitted cupboards, sink unit, electric hob, wall-mounted electric oven, plumbing for washing machine, door to communal gardens.

Bathroom: Gold taps, shower unit, green suite, glazed window to rear.

Study: Glass chandelier, wooden floor.

Exercise 6

Welcome to Boscombe Zoo

- Circus spectacular show twice a day
- See the animals being fed
- Cuddle baby lambs and goats
- Restaurant and cafe open all day
- Take a train ride round the zoo

Open every day except Christmas Day

Exercise 7

Stanley Road Hospital Trust

The following opportunity has arisen for a clear thinking, caring individual to join our acclaimed Trust as a full-time assistant.

For the post, we are looking for an exceptional person. You will help trained nurses assess need and deliver care to the many older patients at our brand new Saltwood Annexe. You must have first-aid training, good communication skills, be patient and caring and enjoy working flexibly.

To apply, please send us a full C.V. together with the names of two referees.

For further information, write to Marion Hobbs, Saltwood Annexe, Webleton Hospital, Grundy Close, Chesterham. Or phone her on 0166778 2349.

Exercise 8

SEE-RIGHT-THROUGH DOUBLE GLAZING

Who can you trust to install double glazing?

Few people are experts in double glazing, So if you're looking to improve your home with PVC-U windows, doors or a conservatory – and don't fancy entrusting such a major decision to a possible cowboy – use SEE-RIGHT-THROUGH.

We use only the best materials, and there's a free 20-year guarantee.

1. We are fast

2. We are careful

3. We leave the site tidy

4. We are the best.

Call now on Freephone 0800 444555 for a no-strings quotation.

One call and you will be in touch with a nationwide network of approved, fully trained installers who are monitored regularly by a team of inspectors.

> SEE-RIGHT-THROUGH
>
> The name to trust

3

Exercise 9   Landscombe College Evening Classes

Title	Day	Tutor	Time	Room
Bee-keeping	Monday	Jamie Green	7 – 9 p.m.	B3
Yoga for Beginners	Tuesday	Pat Hurt	6.30 – 8.00 p.m.	Hall
Computing for Beginners	Thursday	Howard Maynard	3 – 5 p.m.	C14
Advanced Yoga	Wednesday	Pat Hurt	7 – 9 p.m.	Hall
Car Mechanics	Wednesday	Jack Byrne	6 – 8 p.m.	Workshop
Watercolour painting	Tuesday	Nancy Smythe	2 – 4 p.m.	B9

New students may like to know that the following videos acquired by the College are relevant to this term's classes and may be available for hire.

Title	Presenter	Hire charge	Length	Available
Yoga For All	The Graceful Goddess	£1.50	110 mins	On loan
Know Your Car	Ray B. Wise	£3.00	90 mins	Yes
Bees For Life	William & Sarah Price	£2.50	150 mins	Yes
Keeping Bees	Walter Mitts	£1.50	90 mins	On loan

Exercise 10   A table listing PC software might look as shown:

Name	Publisher	Description	Age Range	Date
Encarta	Microsoft	Encyclopaedia	5+	1998
Body Works	PC Advisor	3D journey through the body	7+	2000
Age of Empires	Microsoft	Strategy game	7+	1999
Zoombinis	Broderbund	Maths games	8+	1999
Cartoon Studio	Softkey	Cartoon making kit	6+	1997
Voicepad	Softkey	Voice-enabling word processing	10+	1997

Exercise 11

Make	Type	Price	Colour
Miele	oven	£153.99	black
Electrolux	fridge-freezer	£245.00	white
Tricity	cooker hood	£76.99	silver
Servis	dishwasher	£196.50	brown
Philips	washing machine	£279.99	white
Hoover	upright vacuum cleaner	£89.00	red

Exercise 12

CLASS MARKS 2000

First Name	Surname	Maths	Science	English	Per cent	Total
Janet	Brown-Smythe	40	35	38	75.33	113
Peter	Smith	23	38	46	71.33	107
Richard	Wellington	31	48	40	79.33	119
Danielle-Celeste	Courvoisier	23	44	19	57.33	86
Harry	Longbottom	15	23	37	50.00	75
John	Baker	38	26	22	57.33	86
Mary	French	50	50	50	100.00	150

Exercise 13   Applying styles (your machine may have quite different style formats).

Home Decorating Ltd

To: *Denise Watermill, Marketing Manager*

From: *Arnold Morton, Ceramics Department*

Copied to: *Head of Purchasing*

Subject: <u>Bali and Hong Kong</u>

Date: (today's)

With regard to the recent sales, I am writing to let you know that there was a huge demand for the new lines we purchased from Bali and Hong Kong. Many customers asked when we would be stocking smaller items such as soup bowls, spoons and tea cups, and I feel such items would almost walk off the shelves if we had them in stock.

I suggest we have a meeting as soon as is practicable to discuss purchasing more items from the Far East, and a possible television advertising campaign to accompany these new goods.

Exercise 14   Your merged memo might look like this:

To: David Holmes, IT Department

From: My Name

Date: 2 July 2002

Subject: End of Year Party

As spokesperson for the course, I am writing to ask you to come to our final session in the Staff Room on Friday at 2.00 p.m. We would like to hold a party as a fun way to end the course, and would like you to bring some pizza as a small contribution.

Please let me know if you are unable to attend.

Exercise 15   Your letters should look something like this:

Mr James Smith
York

Date: (today's)

Dear Mr Smith

Extra payment

As a resident of York who has reached the age of 62 and who has been living in the city for 2 years, we have the power to pay you an extra £2,400.

This will be sent in the form of a cheque to your home address at the end of the month.

Yours sincerely

Gordon Best
On behalf of the Inland Revenue

Spreadsheets

ANSWERS TO INTRODUCTORY EXERCISES

Exercise 1

DARTS				
Name	Score 1	Score 2	Score 3	Final score
Marigold	8	11	3	22
Harry	12	22	6	40
Steve	3	9	18	30
David	18	16	5	39
Joan	9	12	11	32
Elizabeth-Jane	11	15	20	46

Exercise 2

SHOPPING			
Item	Cost (£)	Number bought	Final price (£)
Catfood	0.4	10	4
Milk	0.38	6	2.28
Loaf	0.87	2	1.74
Marmalade	1.15	1	1.15
Pasta	0.49	3	1.47
Melon	1.3	2	2.6
Lemonade	0.89	3	2.67

Exercise 3

SHOPPING AT SUPERMART			
Item	Cost (£)	Number bought	Final price (£)
Catfood	£0.40	10	£4.00
Milk	£0.38	6	£2.28
Loaf	£0.93	2	£1.86
Marmalade	£1.35	1	£1.35
Pasta	£0.49	3	£1.47
Melon	£1.30	2	£2.60
Lemonade	£0.89	3	£2.67
Total			£16.23

Exercise 4

Shares					
Months	Bellings	Thatchers	Gordington	Lowden	Morgan
Jan	£2.40	£12.60	£24.00	£0.50	£18.00
Feb	£3.70	£13.20	£14.60	£0.96	£16.50
Mar	£1.60	£7.90	£18.00	£1.30	£17.00
Apr	£0.75	£6.40	£30.30	£4.10	£17.80
May	£4.90	£14.10	£31.70	£3.70	£16.40
Total	£13.35	£54.20	£118.60	£10.56	£85.70
Average	£2.7	£10.8	£23.7	£2.1	£17.1

Exercise 5

Restaurant		
Item	**ME**	FRIEND
Melon	£1.25	
Soup		£1.00
Steak & kidney pie	£4.50	£4.50
Chips	£0.80	
Jacket potato		£0.75
Salad	£1.25	£1.25
Ice-cream	£0.95	
Fruit salad		£0.90
Coffee	£1.70	£0.85
TOTAL	£10.45	£9.25

Exercise 6

Own Brand Cereal Prices					
Comparison					
SHOP	*Gateway*	*Tesco*	*Asda*	*Co-op*	*Safeway*
Size of pack (gm)	500	450	1000	1000	1500
Price per pack	£2.50	£2.00	£3.50	£4.50	£3.75
Cost per 100 gm	£0.50	£0.44	£0.35	£0.45	£0.25

Exercise 7

PETTY CASH EXPENSES					
Dates	**Postage**	**Coffee/Tea**	**Cleaning**	**Furniture**	**Stationery/Disks**
January	£13.50	£11.00	£14.00		£15.75
February	£7.65	£3.50	£14.00		£17.38
March	£19.38	£3.45	£14.00	£385.00	£20.75
April	£9.23	£4.15	£14.00		£9.50
May	£11.68	£2.17	£17.00	£37.99	£12.45
Totals	£61.44	£24.27	£73.00	£422.99	£75.83

4

Exercise 8

Holiday Bookings							
Date of Booking	**Surname**	**Villa**	**Start date**	**End date**	**Max. number**	**Price**	**Price per person**
2/2/02	Browning	Caprice	01-Jun	08-Jun	5	£209	£41.80
25/2/02	Derbyshire	Miramar	15-Jun	22-Jun	4	£354	£88.50
3/3/02	Winslow	Capri	25-May	01-Jun	6	£567	£94.50
15/3/02	Harris	Nuit	15-Jun	22-Jun	3	£295	£98.33
16/4/02	Pentford	Soleil	18-May	25-Jun	4	£680	£170.00
TOTAL						£2,105	
Holiday Bookings							

Exercise 9

Pizza				
Item	Quantity for 2	Quantity for 30	Cost per item	Final Price for 2
Strong flour (lb)	1.50	22.50	£0.70	£1.05
Yeast (sachet)	1.00	15.00	£0.20	£0.20
Fat (oz)	2.00	30.00	£0.40	£0.80
Olive oil (tbs)	3.00	45.00	£0.30	£0.90
Tomatoes	2.00	30.00	£0.25	£0.50
Mozzarella (oz)	6.00	90.00	£0.80	£4.80
Spicy sausage (oz)	4.00	60.00	£0.85	£3.40
Onion	1.00	15.00	£0.30	£0.30
Total				£11.95

Exercise 10   TVs

Make	Price	Size of screen (ins)	Teletext	Features	No. in Stock
Westwood	£159.99	20	Yes	Stereo	20
Jacksons	£198.75	14	Yes	Televideo	14
Merit	£229.99	14	Yes	DVD-player	2
Piccolo	£99.99	14	Yes	Silver	12
Bradleys	£179.00	17	Yes	Silver	5
Clerical	£79.99	2.3	No	Pocket-size	8
Total	£947.71				
Average	£157.95				

Exercise 11   Writer's Costs

MONTH	PENS	PAPER	TRAVEL	DISKS	COFFEE	TOTAL
JAN	£2.50	£3.70	£15.34	£1.80	£0.65	£24
FEB	£3.67	£9.50	£7.78	£3.50	£2.40	£27
MAR	£1.80	£2.70	£12.90	£4.85	£2.50	£25
APR	£5.50	£0.00	£22.50	£2.70	£0.90	£32
MAY	£2.00	£3.45	£5.00	£1.10	£2.45	£14
Overall Total						£121
Average						£24

Exercise 12

Food	Price(£)	Discount offered
Omelette	£4.50	£0.23
Salad	£2.00	£0.10
Chips	£1.50	£0.08
Fudge cake	£2.75	£0.14
Tea	£0.85	£0.04
Total	£11.60	£0.58
Final Price	£11.02	
Discount is:		
5%		

Exercise 13 **Sale of Tiles for January**

Code number	Colour	Price of pack	Cost of 1 tile	Packs sold	Final price
005	Red	£6.50	£0.13	20	£130.00
026	Yellow	£12.45	£0.25	14	£174.30
041	Black	£8.75	£0.18	35	£306.25
018	Green	£7.95	£0.16	30	£238.50
019	Green	£18.45	£0.37	10	£184.50
006	Patterned-Brown	£3.25	£0.07	25	£81.25
TOTAL				134	£1,114.80
No. tiles per pack	50				

Exercise 14 New Carpets

Room	Length (ft)	Width (ft)	Area (sq ft)	Area (sq metres)	Cost (sq metres)	Final Price
Sitting	14.00	10.50	147.00	13.66	£22.85	£311.36
Bed	9.00	8.25	74.25	6.90	£19.25	£132.78
Bath	6.00	7.00	42.00	3.90	£8.00	£31.21
Total						£475.36

4

ANSWERS TO ADVANCED EXERCISES

Exercise 1

Charity Contributions								
Charity	Percent	Jan	Feb	March	April	May	June	Average
RNIB	50%	£1,000	£1,840	£645	£2,500	£2,340	£1,158	£1,581
Birds	12%	£240	£442	£155	£600	£562	£278	£379
Lifeboats	5%	£100	£184	£64	£250	£234	£116	£158
Sue Ryder	25%	£500	£920	£322	£1,250	£1,170	£579	£790
Oxfam	8%	£160	£294	£103	£400	£374	£185	£253
Total	100%	£2,000	£3,680	£1,289	£5,000	£4,680	£2,315	

Exercise 2

Expenditure over four months					
	1st month	2nd month	3rd month	4th month	Average
Holidays	£0.00	£0.00	£350.00	£0.00	£87.50
Heating	£25.00	£25.00	£25.00	£25.00	£25.00
Food	£75.00	£30.00	£60.00	£45.00	£52.50
Travel	£5.00	£12.50	£5.00	£2.50	£6.25
Newspapers and magazines	£0.75	£0.75	£0.75	£0.75	£0.75
Clothes	£65.00	£13.45	£48.00	£7.00	£33.36
Total	£170.75	£81.50	£138.75	£80.25	
Income	£200.00	£245.00	£200.00	£200.00	
Remaining money	£29.25	£163.30	£61.25	£119.75	

Exercise 3

Temperature °C							
	Jan	Feb	Mar	Apr	May	Jun	Average
Oxford	3.70	4.20	5.80	8.40	11.70	14.90	8.12
Lyneham	3.90	3.50	6.00	7.70	11.10	14.10	7.72
Cambridge	3.40	3.90	5.70	8.30	11.60	14.70	7.93
Sheffield	3.80	3.90	5.40	7.80	10.90	14.10	7.65
Durham	2.80	3.20	4.60	6.80	9.60	12.90	6.65
AVERAGE	3.52	3.74	5.50	7.80	10.98	14.14	7.61

Exercise 4

BOAT HIRE					
No. of people	1 Day	2 Day	3 Day	Weekly	Average
2 – standard class	£80.00	£120.00	£180.00	£240.00	£34
2 – superior class	£100.00	£130.00	£250.00	£280.00	£40
Autumn special – 2 superior	£90.00	£125.00	£200.00	£265.00	£38
4 – superior class	£150.00	£180.00	£225.00	£300.00	£43
6 – luxury	£200.00	£225.00	£250.00	£375.00	£54
8 – standard	£210.00	£300.00	£330.00	£360.00	£51

Exercise 5   Data sorted alphabetically by type, then by ascending order of price.

	A	B	C	D	E	F
1	Type	Bedrooms	Garage	Garden	Price	Location
2	Bungalow	2	Yes	Patio garde	£75,799	Selby
3	Bungalow	3	Yes	Yes	£175,000	Selby
4	Detached	5	Double	Marina	£300,990	Selby
5	Flat	3	No	Yes	£97,000	York
6	Flat	4	Yes	No	£100,000	York
7	Flat	1	No	No	£115,000	Sheffield
8	Semidetached	3	Yes	Yes	£200,450	York
9	Semidetached	4	Yes	Paddock	£217,950	Derby

Exercise 6   Database sorted in ascending order of Kcals per 100g.

Item	Weight (g)	Kcals	Fat	Protein	Kcals per 100 g	Fat per 100 g	Protein per 100 g
Baked beans	420	260	1.20	19.40	61.90	0.29	4.62
Tuna	132	120	0.28	28.00	90.91	0.21	21.21
Dried apricots	500	800	3.00	20.70	160.00	0.60	4.14
Sardines	90	156	8.10	20.70	173.33	9.00	23.00
Peanut butter	340	2023	172.72	83.64	595.00	50.80	24.60
Almonds	300	1842	150.00	63.30	614.00	50.00	21.10
The item of food with the least Kcals per 100 g is baked beans.							

Exercise 7   The 2D column chart 'Final results in 1999':

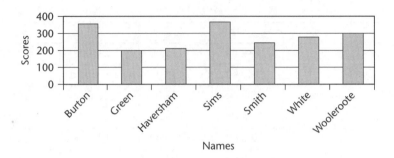

Exercise 8   The pie chart showing comparative pen costs for one pen:

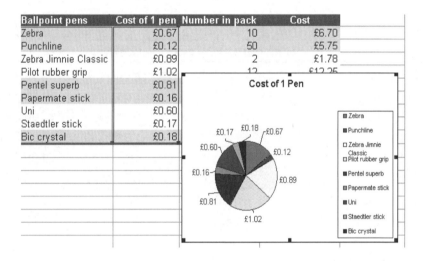

Ballpoint pens	Cost of 1 pen	Number in pack	Cost
Zebra	£0.67	10	£6.70
Punchline	£0.12	50	£5.75
Zebra Jimnie Classic	£0.89	2	£1.78
Pilot rubber grip	£1.02	12	£12.25
Pentel superb	£0.81		
Papermate stick	£0.16		
Uni	£0.60		
Staedtler stick	£0.17		
Bic crystal	£0.18		

Exercise 9   The original chart (step 6):

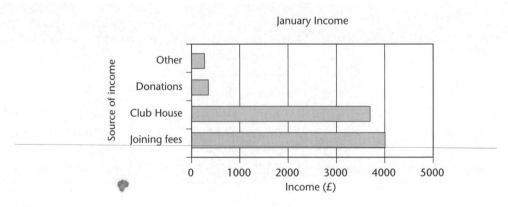

After amending (step 8):

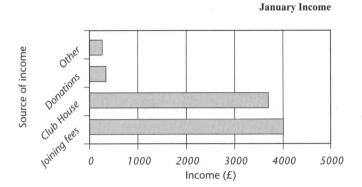

As a pie chart (step 9):

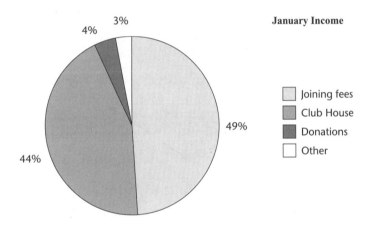

Comparative chart (step 11):

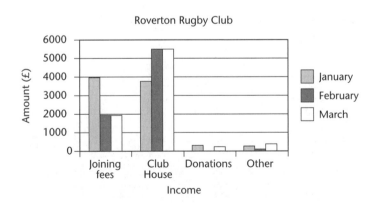

Exercise 10   The final version of the column chart (step 5):

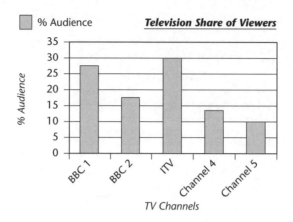

Exercise 11   The original line graph (step 6):

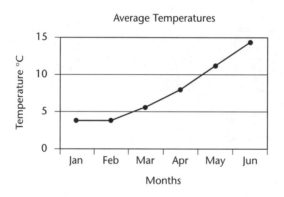

Comparative column chart showing the temperatures for January to June (step 8):

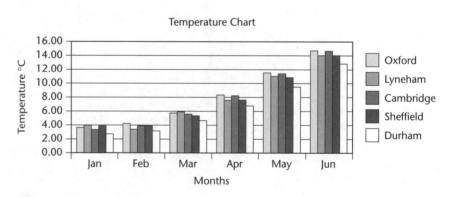

Exercise 12   Pie chart showing students' overall percentage marks (step 5):

Class Marks 2002

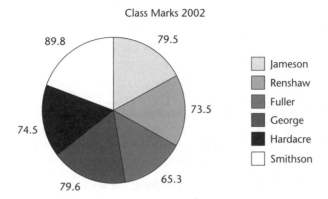

Bar chart with scale adjusted (step 6):

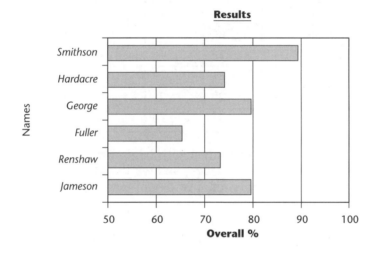

Exercise 13

Chalfont Senior School
West Widnes
Harnaton
HA15 3XP

[today's date]

Dear Parent

You will be pleased to learn that our 6th Form boys have done very well this term. They all sat their English, French and Mathematics examinations and have gained higher marks than the same set last year.

You may like to see the full details of their results and so these are set out below:

Name	English	French	Mathematics	Total	Overall %
Jameson	34	18	26	78	79.6
Renshaw	26	15	31	72	73.5
Fuller	25	16	23	64	65.3
George	31	19	28	78	79.6
Hardacre	29	21	23	73	74.5
Smithson	35	20	33	88	89.8

As you can see from the chart, Nigel Smithson fully justifies the prize for academic success and we look forward to seeing you at the award ceremony on the last day of term.

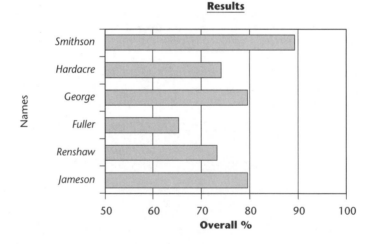

Results

Yours faithfully

Charles Belham
Headmaster

Exercise 14 Stacked comparative chart showing tennis and football only (step 5):

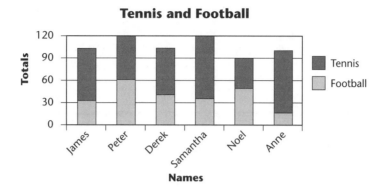

Chart showing the average scores for all sports (step 7):

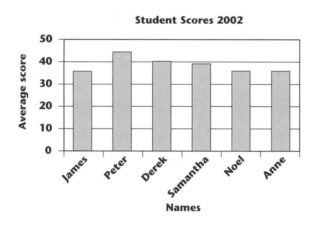

Exercise 15

ITEM	TEST 1 %	TEST 2 %	TEST 3 %	AVERAGE OVERALL SCORE	FINAL RESULT
Cheese	56	45	71	57	disliked
Pork sausage	67	93	87	82	liked
Chocolate	78	61	67	69	liked
Dried fruit	34	54	23	37	disliked
Steak	82	87	73	81	liked
Tomato	54	65	38	52	disliked
Red wine	78	76	65	73	liked

Databases

ANSWERS TO INTRODUCTORY EXERCISES

Exercise 1   The Food database:

Recipes : Table	
Field Name	**Data Type**
▶ Main food	Text
Title	Text
Cooking (mins)	Number
Portions	Number
Calories	Number

Exercise 2   The Sailings database, with the field names Bicycle supplement and Fast supplement added:

sailing costs : Table	
Field Name	**Data Type**
Dates	Text
UK Port	Text
French port	Text
Short stay (£)	Currency
Long stay (£)	Currency
Weekend extra (£)	Currency
Bicycle supplement	Currency
▶ Fast supplement	Currency

Exercise 3   The Recipes table of records:

Main food	Title	Cooking (mins)	Portions	Calories
Cod	Cod with herbs	50	4	193
Tuna	Tuna bean salad	12	4	185
Red pepper	Roast vegetable soup	90	8	150
Pasta	Pasta with pesto sauce	30	4	538
Eggs	Chocolate souffle	30	8	204
Banana	Banana ice-cream	10	4	250
*		0	0	0

Record: |◄ ◄ 6 ► ►| ►* of 6

Exercise 4   The Chairs table:

Microsoft Access - [Chairs : Table]

File Edit View Insert Format Records Tools Window Help

Name	Price	Discount offered	Colours available	Code
Adjustable typist	£19.99	☑	4	TEK
Delux gas-lift typist	£43.99	☑	6	1116
Bentwood operator	£69.99	☐	1	WDOPR
Contemporary operator	£69.99	☐	2	AGNELLO
Modern operator	£59.99	☑	4	BETA
Ergonomic	£149.99	☑	7	VKHBA
Multifunctional	£119.99	☐	5	1228
Continuous use	£179.99	☐	3	HCT

Exercise 5   The Bikes table after deleting the Rocket Goldie entry:

Make	Price (£)	Type	CC	Year	Details
AJS	5999	Big port	350	1927	Black finish
Ariel	1750	Leader	250	1963	Clock
BSA	5999	DB34	500	1954	TLS front brake
AJS	2350	185	500	1957	Crhome tank panels
Ariel	3750	VH Red Hunter	500	1954	Excellent condition
Ariel	1950	Leader	250	1961	red finish
*	0		0	0	

Exercise 6   The Furniture database sorted in alphabetical order of name:

	Name	Price	Discount offered	Colours available	Code
	Adjustable typist	£19.99	☑	4	TEK
	Bentwood operator	£69.99	☐	1	WDOPR
	Contemporary operator	£69.99	☐	2	AGNELLO
	Continuous use	£179.99	☐	3	HCT
	Delux gas-lift typist	£43.99	☑	6	1116
	Ergonomic	£149.99	☑	7	VKHBA
	Modern operator	£59.99	☑	4	BETA
🖉	Multifunctional	£0.00	☐	6	1228
✳		£0.00	☐	0	

Chairs : Table

Exercise 7   The Sailing costs table sorted alphabetically by French port:

month	UK Port	French port	Short stay (£)	Long stay (£)	Weekend extr	Bicycle supple
March	Portsmouth	Caen	£110.00	£146.00	£13.50	£5.00
Spt	Portsmouth	Caen	£62.00	£87.00	£8.00	£0.00
July	Plymouth	Roscoff	£133.00	£173.00	£16.00	£9.00
Aug	Plymouth	Roscoff	£121.00	£152.00	£13.50	£5.00
Spt	Plymouth	Roscoff	£65.00	£90.00	£8.00	£0.00
March	Portsmouth	St. Malo	£126.00	£166.00	£13.50	£5.00
July	Portsmouth	St. Malo	£145.00	£189.00	£16.00	£9.00

sailing costs : Table

Record: 1 of 7

Exercise 8   Primary key set on Class code and properties of Start time amended:

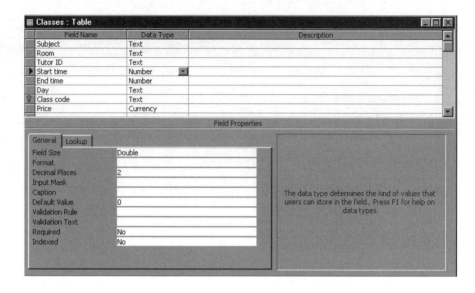

Exercise 9   Composers table sorted on descending order of year born:

Composer	Initials	Title	Key	Year born	Nationality	Price of CD	Code
Chopin	F	Piano concerto no. 1	E minor	1810	Polish	3.99	C7
Schubert	F	Unfinished Symphony	B minor	1797	Austrian	2.95	S3
Beethoven	L. Van	Choral Symphony	D minor	1770	German	2.5	B5
Mozart	W.A.	Salzburg Symphony no. 2	B flat major	1756	Austrian	5.35	M6
Bach	J.S.	Brandenburg Concerto no 1	F major	1685	German	8.99	B9
Vivaldi	A	Spring	E major	1675	Italian	2.49	V2
				0		0	

Exercise 10   Records filtered to find only those rated 4:

Title	Price (£)	Minimum age	Website	Rating
Games 3	10	7	www.tivola.co.uk	4
Pop-up Dictionary	30	7	www.oup.co.uk	4
Physicus	18	8	www.tivola.co.uk	4
*	0	0		0

Record: 14 ◄ | 1 | ► ►I ►* | of 3 (Filtered)

Results of filtering to find CD-ROMs for the under nines costing less than £20:

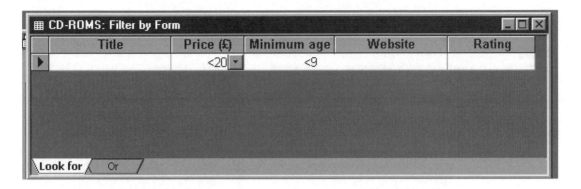

Exercise 11   Filter by Form:

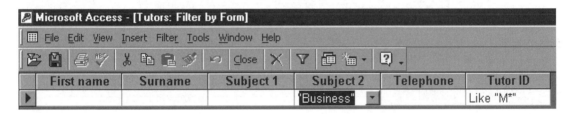

Exercise 12   The Sailing costs table filtered to find short stays from Portsmouth costing £90–£130:

month	UK Port	French port	Short stay (£)	Long stay (£)	Weekend extr	Bicycle supp
March	Portsmouth	St. Malo	£126.00	£166.00	£13.50	£5.0
March	Portsmouth	Caen	£110.00	£146.00	£13.50	£5.0
*			£0.00	£0.00	£0.00	£0.0

Record: 14 ◀ 1 ▶ ▶I ▶* of 2 (Filtered)

Exercise 13   The Composers table sorted to find recordings costing less than £5 that were written by a German or Austrian composer:

Composer	Initials	Title	Key	Year born	Nationality	Price of CD	
Schubert	F	Unfinished Symphony	B minor	1797	Austrian	2.95	S3
Beethoven	L. Van	Choral Symphony	D minor	1770	German	2.5	B5

Composers : Table

Exercise 14   Query to find late summer activities:

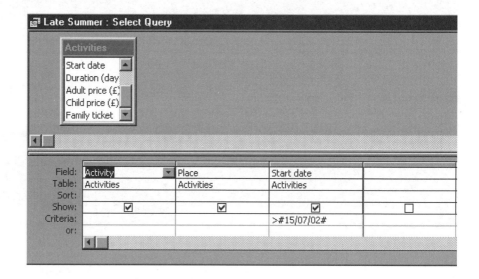

The results:

Late Summer : Select Query

Activity	Place	Start date
Open day	Ramsgate Harbour	30/07
Arthurian antics	Pickering Castle	04/08
King for a day	Legoland	25/07
Puppet Picnic	Grey's Court, Henley	30/07

Record: 1 of 4

Exercise 15   Query to find chairs costing more than £120:

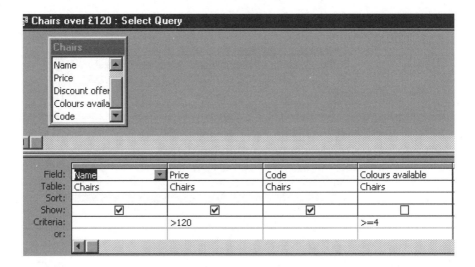

The results:

Name	Price	Code
Ergonomic	£149.99	VKHBA
Comfort	£189.99	COMFORT
Ultimate Executive	£229.99	BBAS
*	£0.00	

Exercise 16   Recipes that take less than 15 minutes to cook:

Quick recipes : Select Query

Main food	Title	Cooking (mins)
Tuna	Tuna bean salad	12
Banana	Banana ice-cream	10
*		0

5

ANSWERS TO ADVANCED EXERCISES

Exercise 1   Table searched for senior males:

Senior Males : Select Query		
Firstname	**Surname**	**Joining Date**
▶ Francis	Bergot	18-Jun-01
Peter	Brown	28-Jun-01
Graham	Harper	04-Jul-01
Martin	Piller	15-Aug-01
Harold	Wilson	22-Jun-01
*		

Exercise 2   There are three classes that cost between £20 and £30:

Classes from £20 to £30 : Select Query			
Subject	**Day**	**Start time**	**End time**
▶ French	Wed	7	9
Spanish	Fri	7	9
Business	Fri	2	4.3
*		0	0

Exercise 3   AutoForm for the Books table

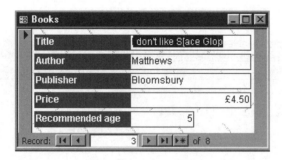

Exercise 4   Deleting a record:

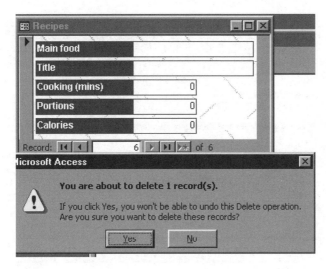

Wizard recipe form:

Main food	Title	Cooking (mins)	Portion number	Calories
Red pepper	Roast vegetable soup	90	8	150
Tuna	Tuna bean salad	12	4	185
Cod	Cod with herbs	50	4	193
Eggs	Chocolate souffle	30	8	204
Pasta	Pasta with pesto sauce	30	4	538

Exercise 5   Result of Query to find joining date of all seniors:

Seniors : Select Query

Surname	Membership No	Joining Date
Brown	1	24-May-01
Bergot	4	18-Jun-01
Wilson	5	22-Jun-01
Brown	6	28-Jun-01
Harper*	9	04-Jul-01
Piller	12	15-Aug-01

Record: 1 of 6

5

Exercise 6 Designing a query to find all chairs aimed at executives or operators:

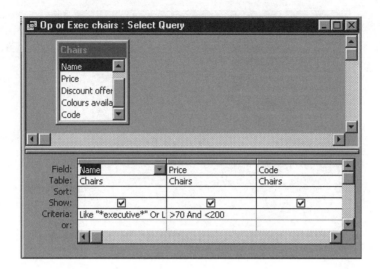

The result:

Op or Exec chairs

Name	*Price*	*Code*
Wood Executive	£169.99	1314A5

Exercise 7 Pre-1962 bike report (step 4):

pre-1962 bikes

Make	Price (£)	Type	CC	Details
AJS	2350	185	500	Chrome tank panels
Ariel	3750	VH Red Hunter	500	Excellent condition
Ariel	1950	Leader	250	red finish

Exercise 8   Report based on a query for female club members

Female members

Firstname	Surname	Joining Date	Category
Joan	Brown	24-May-01	Senior
Madge	Brown	22-May-01	Junior
Diane	Brown	28-Jun-01	Junior
Susan	Hill	01-Jul-01	Concession
Sally	Harper	04-Jul-01	Junior
Shirley	Webb	03-Aug-01	Concession

Exercise 9   Report grouped by age:

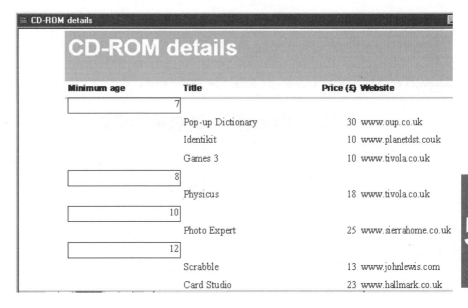

Exercise 10   Grouped report showing average salaries:

job details

Location	Employer	Job	Salary	Closing date
Abingdon				
	Beaumont House	Care Assistant	£12,500.00	14/02/02
	Garsington	Education Officer	£14,000.00	14/02/02

Summary for 'Location' = Abingdon (2 detail records)
Avg   £13,250.00

Oxford				
	Mango	Administrator	£17,500.00	20/02/02
	Hedges	Secretary	£17,950.00	01/03/02
	Connell	Sales	£18,000.00	20/02/02

Summary for 'Location' = Oxford (3 detail records)
Avg   £17,816.67

Witney				
	Gateway Hotel	2nd chef	£19,000.00	05/03/02

Exercise 11   The reformatted Recipe AutoForm:

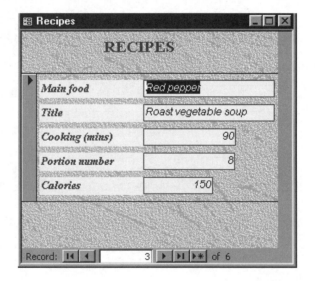

Exercise 12

Exercise 13   Average report customized:

Job Details

Location	Employer	Job	Salary	Closing date
Abingdon				
	Beaumont House	Care Assistant	£12,500.00	14/02/02
	Garsington	Education Officer	£14,000.00	14/02/02
Average salaries			£13,250.00	
Oxford				
	Mango	Administrator	£17,500.00	20/02/02
	Hedges	Secretary	£17,950.00	01/03/02
	Connell	Sales	£18,000.00	20/02/02
Average salaries			£17,816.67	

5

Exercise 14

a) Creating a relationship.

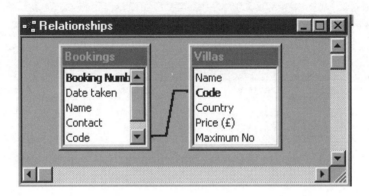

b) The Summer French Villas query.

Bookings.Name	Contact	Month required	Villas.Name	Price (£)
Black	01235 19876	July	Flowers	150
Thomson	01235 67584	June	La Girande	286

MODEL ANSWERS 6

Presentation

ANSWERS TO INTRODUCTORY EXERCISES

Exercise 1

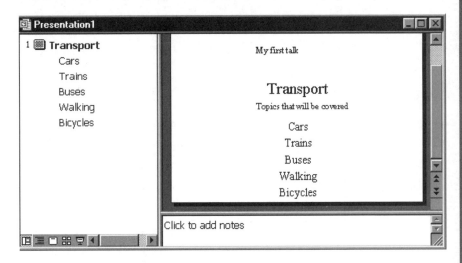

Exercise 2

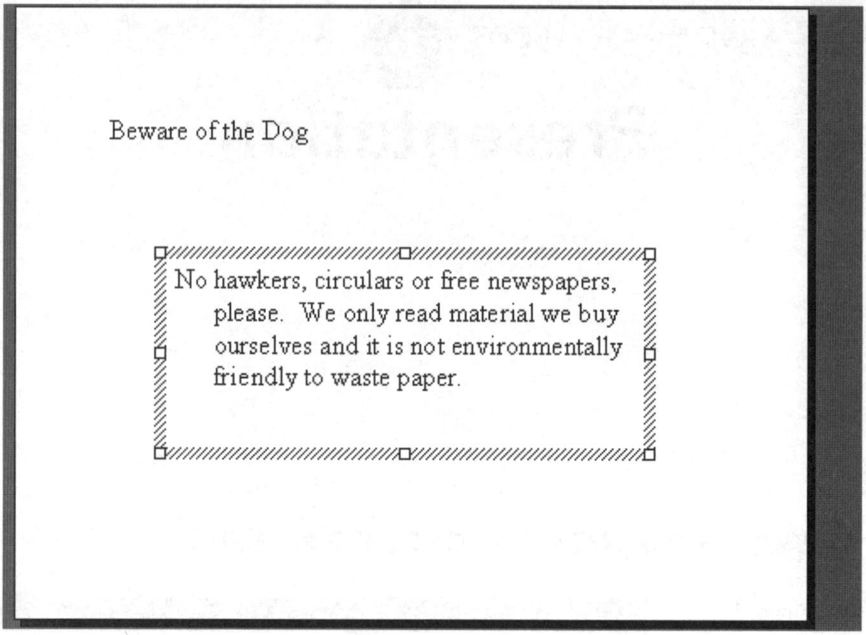

Beware of the Dog

No hawkers, circulars or free newspapers, please. We only read material we buy ourselves and it is not environmentally friendly to waste paper.

Exercise 3

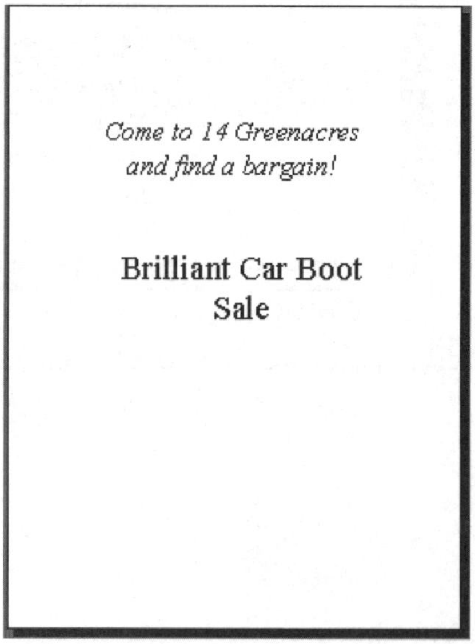

Come to 14 Greenacres and find a bargain!

Brilliant Car Boot Sale

Exercise 4

My first talk

<u>Transport</u>

Topics that will be covered

Cars

Trains

Buses

Walking

Bicycles

Exercise 5

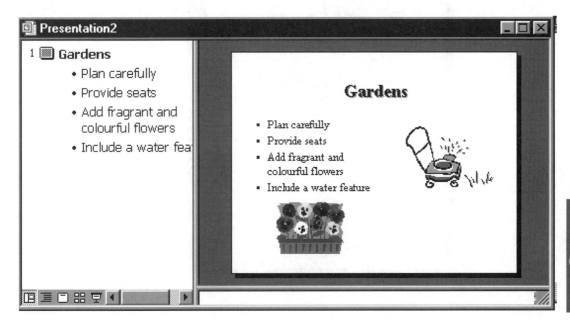

Exercise 6

Beware of the Dog

*No hawkers, circulars or free newspapers,
please. We only read material we buy
ourselves and it is not environmentally
friendly to waste paper.*

Exercise 7

Exercise 8

Exercise 9

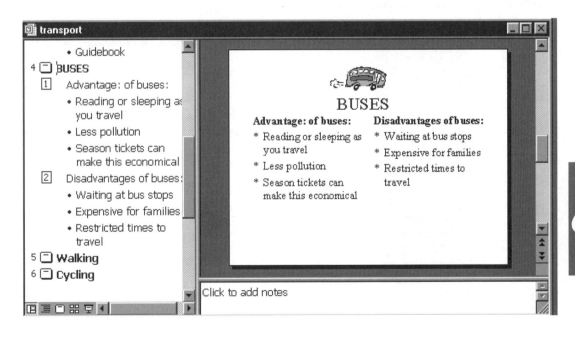

Exercise 10   The flowers slide (step 7):

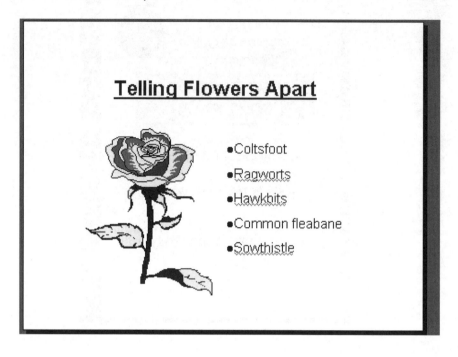

Exercise 11   Changing the text in a slide (step 5)

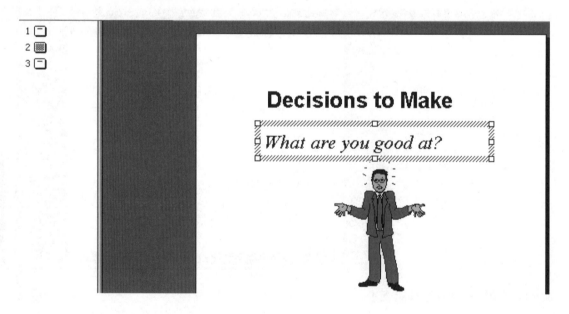

Exercise 12

Exercise 13 Creating a 'get well soon' card.

Exercise 14

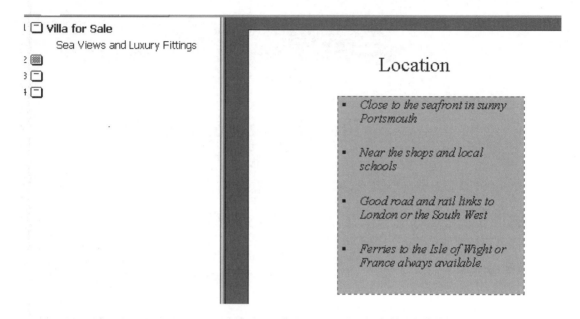

1 ☐ **Villa for Sale**
   Sea Views and Luxury Fittings
2 ▦
3 ☐
4 ☐

Location

- *Close to the seafront in sunny Portsmouth*

- *Near the shops and local schools*

- *Good road and rail links to London or the South West*

- *Ferries to the Isle of Wight or France always available.*

ANSWERS TO ADVANCED EXERCISES

Exercise 1   The notes page:

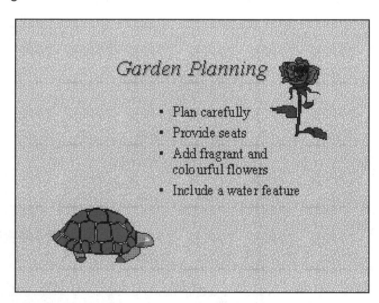

Garden Planning

- Plan carefully
- Provide seats
- Add fragrant and colourful flowers
- Include a water feature

College course starts 19 September
Address for enrolment forms
Book to read: Planning your garden by Deirdre Wiseman

Exercise 2   Adding a picture using AutoShapes:

Exercise 3

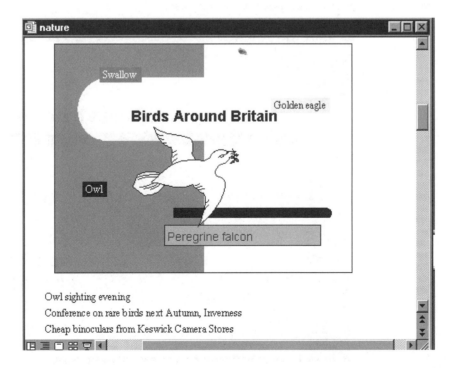

Exercise 4   Applying design templates:

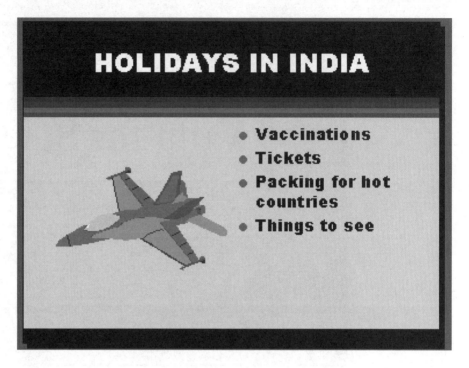

Exercise 5   Customizing design templates:

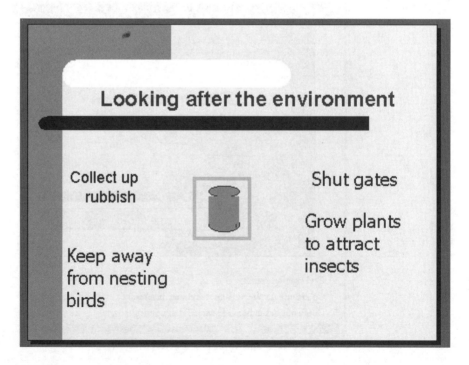

Exercise 6

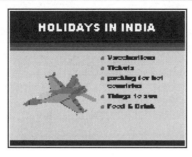

1   2

Exercise 7   Changing the title style using Slide Master:

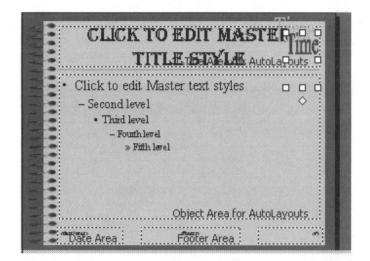

Exercise 8

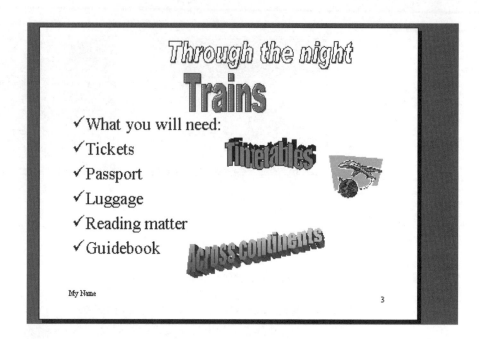

Exercise 9

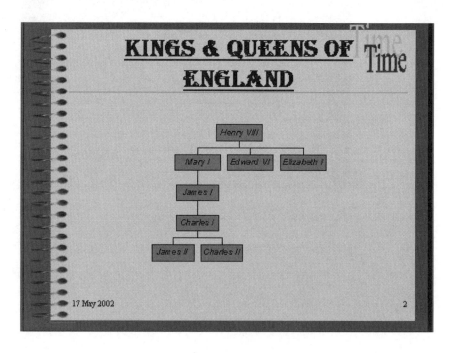

Exercise 10

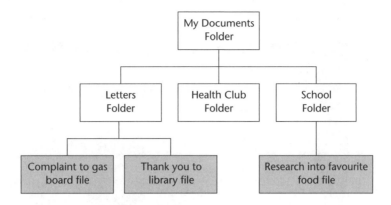

Exercise 11   Creating a column chart:

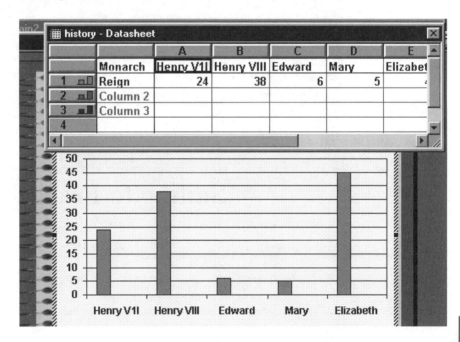

Creating a pie chart:

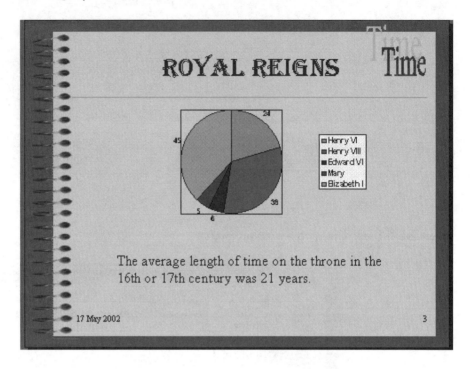

Exercise 12

Sailing to France

Dates	B & B	Standard Hotel	Premium Hotel
Nov - March	£219	£274	£374
March - May	£250	£305	£405
May - July	£280	£335	£490
July - Aug	£294	£349	£504
Sept	£250	£305	£405

Cost of accommodation for 5 nights.

Exercise 14   Setting a transition (Exercise 13 will require a similar process):

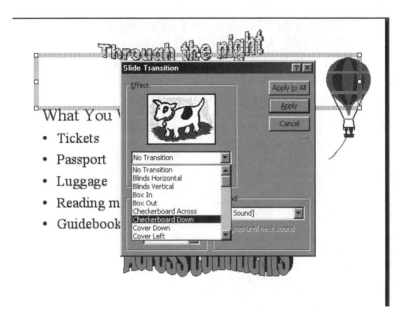

Exercise 15   Animating slides:

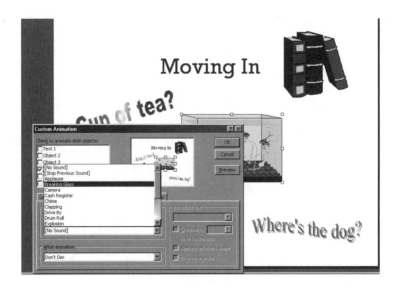

Exercise 16   Creating the presentation outline:

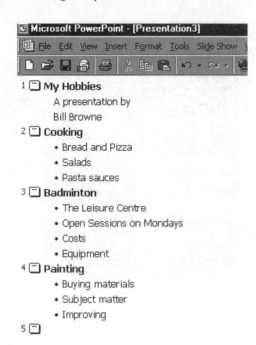

MODEL ANSWERS

7

Information and communication

ANSWERS TO INTRODUCTORY EXERCISES

Exercise 1   Finding what the weather will be like in Sheffield using the BBC Web site:

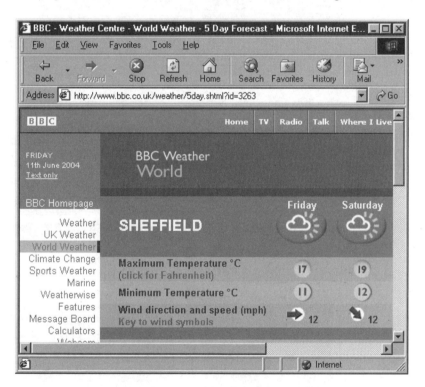

© BBC

Exercise 2   www.laterlife.com holiday page:

www.lifes4living.co.uk holiday page for comparison:

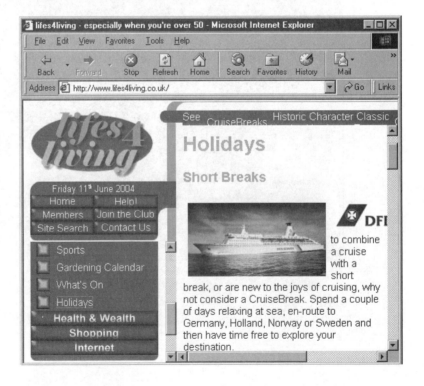

Exercise 3   Online shopping at www.waitrose.com:

Shopping at www.iceland.co.uk:

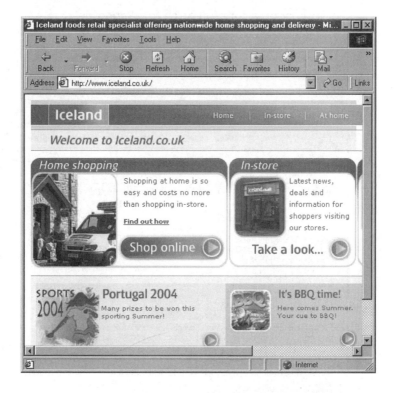

Exercise 4   A place to skate in Milton Keynes was found by going to www.excite.co.uk>directory>Sports>Skating>Ice Skating>Skating Clubs and Rinks:

Reproduced by courtesy of Roy Stubbs and Milton Keynes Ice Skating Club

Exercise 5   Use www.google.com to search for skating rinks:

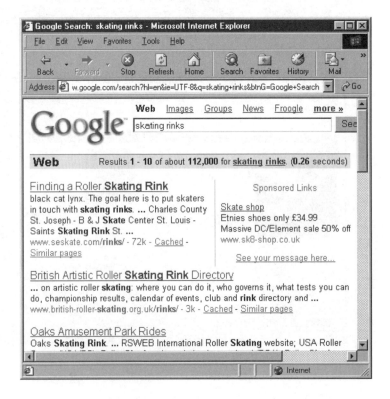

Exercise 6   Following the directory listings on Altavista: Recreation>Pets>Fish and Aquaria> we discovered the Drumanee Aquatics site at www.drumaneeaquatics.co.uk:

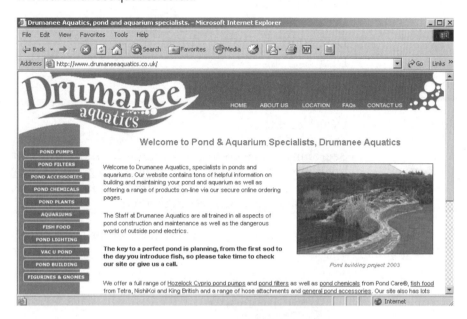

Exercise 7   Details of the opening times of the National Railway Museum, York from www.nrm.org.uk:

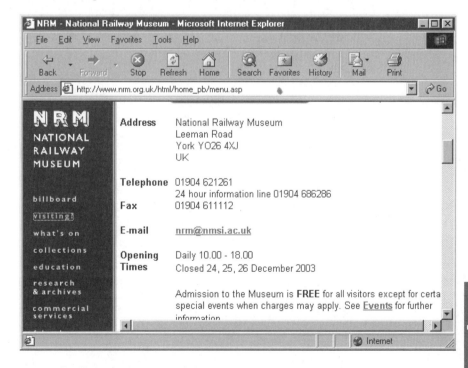

Reproduced courtesy of the National Railway Museum. © Trustees of the Science Museum, 2004

Exercise 8   Adding a Web image to a document:

43 Firtree Road
Beckwith
Derbyshire
DB5 1JT

15 July 2002

Dear Harvey

Searching the Web today I found the most brilliant information on breeding goldfish. The URL is http://members.aol.com/sirchin/gold-fish.htm but I've saved the information and will send it to you by e-mail once I get myself registered.

What do you think of this picture for our newsletter?

All the best

Jan

(Artwork supplied by Lyn Duedall).

Exercise 9   A Website on watercolour painting:

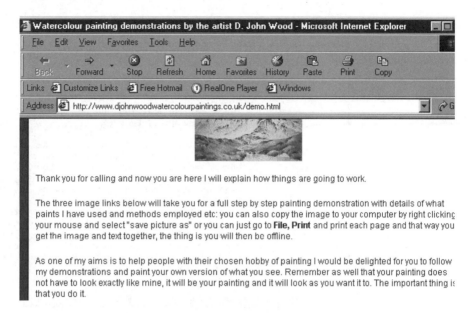

(Artwork supplied by D. John Wood).

Saving the page as a text file:

Opened as a text file:

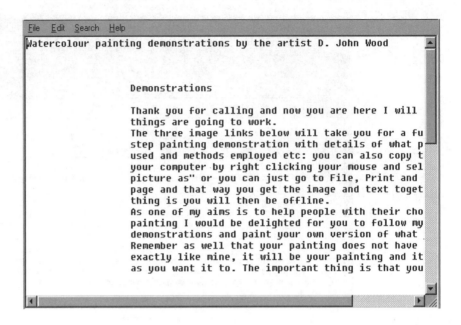

Exercise 10   Pasting information from www.toysrus.co.uk into Word:

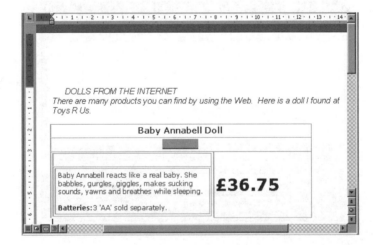

Exercise 11   Saving Web pages:

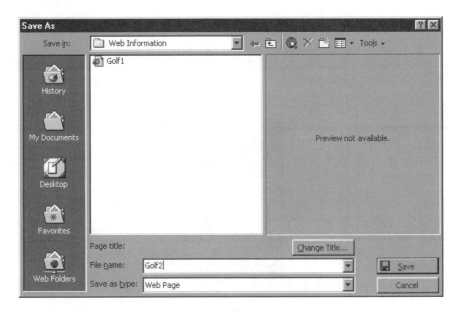

Exercise 12   Organizing favourite Web pages:

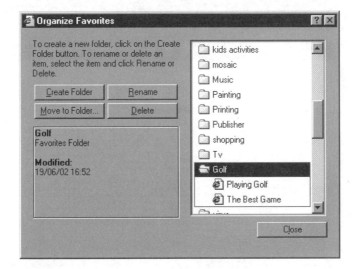

Exercise 13   Selecting the text of a news report:

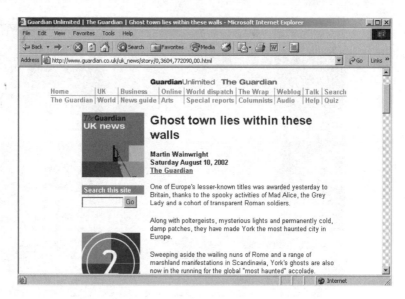

© The Guardian. www.guardian.co.uk

Pasting into Word:

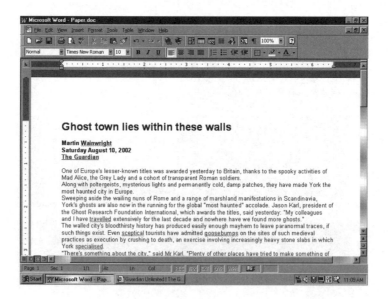

Exercise 14   Results of holiday search on www.firstchoice.co.uk:

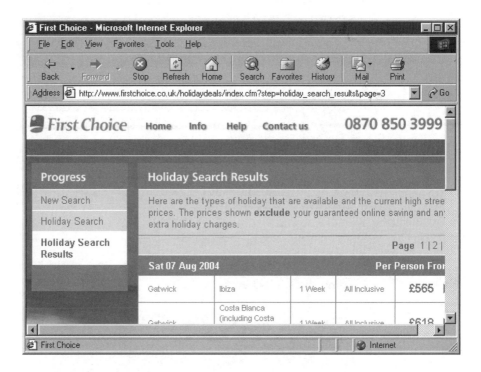

ANSWERS TO ADVANCED EXERCISES

Exercise 1   Writing an e-mail to a friend:

Exercise 2   Writing an e-mail to a TV company:

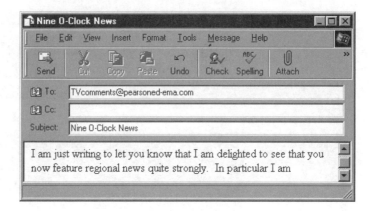

Exercise 3   Using the spell-checker:

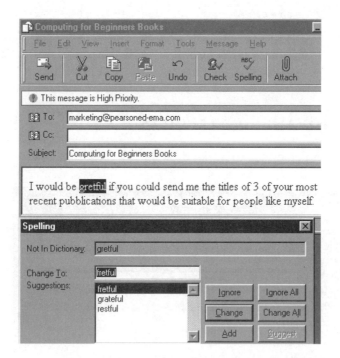

Exercise 4   Forwarding an e-mail:

Exercise 5   Replying to an e-mail:

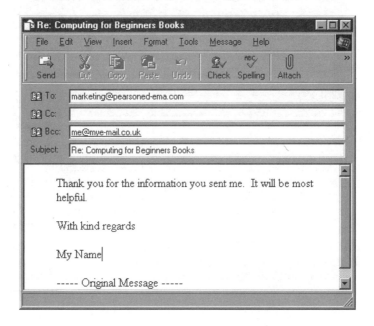

Exercise 6   Copying text between e-mail messages:

Exercise 7   Copying text between applications:

Exercise 8   Entering e-mail addresses in your Address Book:

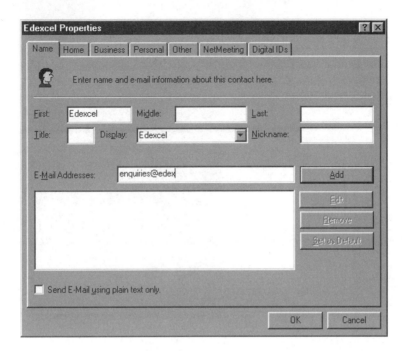

Exercise 9   Creating a group e-mail address:

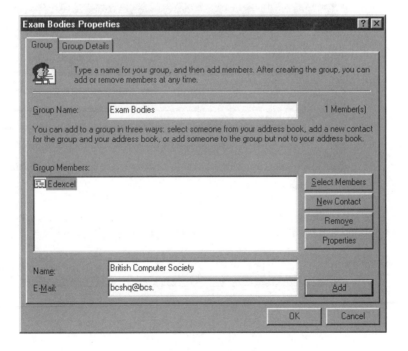

Exercise 10 Marking a message as unread:

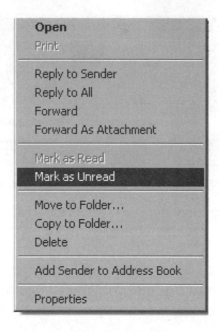

Exercise 11 Attaching a file to an e-mail:

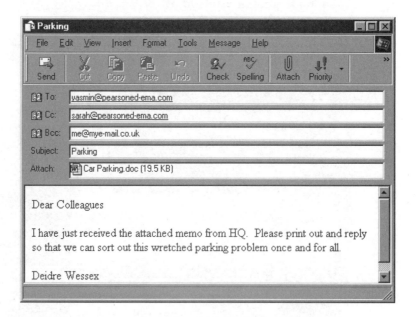

Exercise 12   Attaching another file to an e-mail:

Exercise 13

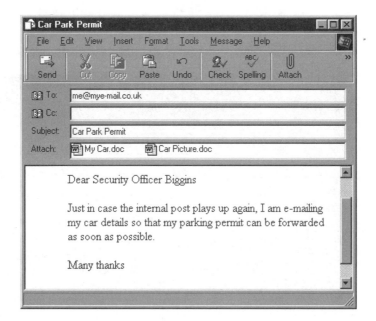

Exercise 14   Creating a new e-mail folder:

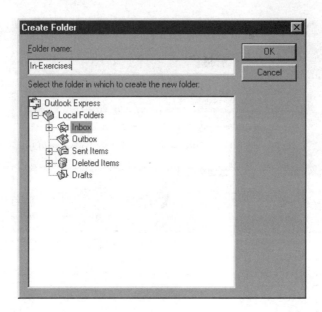

Exercise 15   Finding an e-mail:

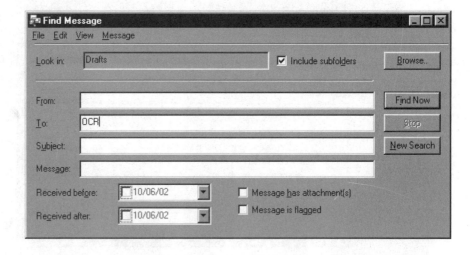

Exercise 16 Crossword solutions:

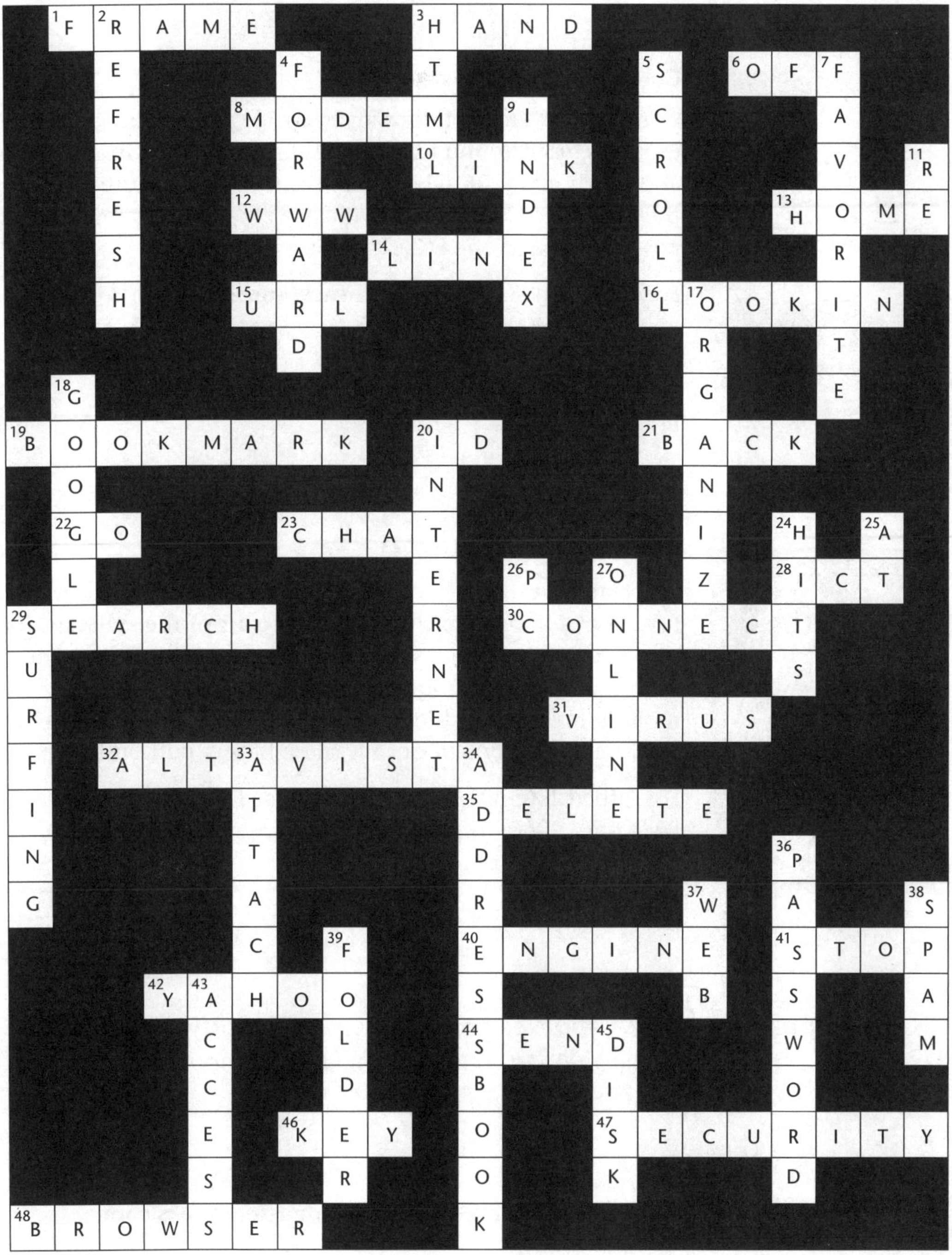

Ideal books to accompany your Practical Exercises text:

Complete Coursebooks

Complete coverage of the syllabus, with lots of detail, examples, exercises, background information, hints and tips from experts, and much more! Ideal both for self-study and for tutor-led courses, the Complete Coursebooks will answer every question you could possibly have on the ECDL syllabus.

For Office 2003: 0131964313 (new for Dec 2004)
For Office 2000: 0130399159
For Office XP: 0130399175
For Office 97: 0131248421
Price: £19.99 – £21.99

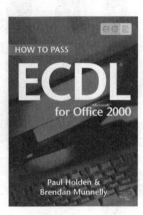

'How to Pass' Workbooks

Especially created for tutor-led courses, these workbooks will take you step-by-step through every part of the syllabus, using many worked examples to make sure you have fully understood each section. Check out the great four colour 'cut-out-and-keep' module reference guides – all the key information on each module, carefully laid out on these handy pull-outs.

For Office 2003: 0131964305 (new for Dec 2004)
For Office 2000: 0131130129
For Office XP: 0131130137
For Office 97: 0131130137
Price: £15.99 – £17.99

*Our books are written and designed to help you **study** for the ECDL, **remember** what you have learned – and **pass** the exams with confidence!*

To order or for more information, visit **www.pearson-books.com**